PRESENTED TO: _____

FROM: _____

DATE: _____

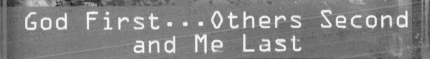

WOMEN

100 DAYS TO A RADICAL CHANGE.

God First...Others Second
and Me Last

The quoted ideas expressed in this book (but not Scripture verses) are not, in all cases, exact quotations, as some have been edited for clarity and brevity. In all cases, the author has attempted to maintain the speaker's original intent. In some cases, quoted material for this book was obtained from secondary sources, primarily print media. While every effort was made to ensure the accuracy of these sources, the accuracy cannot be guaranteed. For additions, deletions, corrections, or clarifications in future editions of this text, please write Freeman-Smith, LLC.

The Holy Bible, King James Version

The Holy Bible, New King James Version (NKJV) Copyright © 1982 by Thomas Nelson, Inc. Used by permission.

New Century Version®. (NCV) Copyright © 1987, 1988, 1991 by Word Publishing, a division of Thomas Nelson, Inc. All rights reserved. Used by permission.

The Holman Christian Standard Bible™ (Holman CSB) Copyright © 1999, 2000, 2001 by Holman Bible Publishers. Used by permission.

The Holy Bible, New International Version®. (NIV) Copyright © 1973, 1978, 1984 International Bible Society. Used by permission of Zondervan. All rights reserved.

The Holy Bible. New Living Translation (NLT) copyright © 1996 Tyndale Charitable Trust. Used by permission of Tyndale House Publishers.

The New American Standard Bible®, (NASB) Copyright © 1960, 1962, 1963, 1968, 1971, 1972, 1973, 1975, 1977, 1995 by The Lockman Foundation. Used by permission.

Scripture taken from The Message. (MSG) Copyright © 1993, 1994, 1995, 1996, 2000, 2001, 2002. Used by permission of NavPress Publishing Group.

Cover Design by Kim Russell / Wahoo Designs
Page Layout by Bart Dawson

ISBN 978-1-60587-241-4

Printed in the United States of America

WOMEN

100 DAYS
TO A
RADICAL
CHANGE.

God First...Others Second
and Me Last

INTRODUCTION

It's a familiar saying, and it's good advice: Put God first, others second, yourself last. But sometimes, amid the grinding pressures of everyday life, we reverse the order. We place ourselves first and others second, leaving God for last if, that is, we take time to think of Him at all.

Have you spent much time thinking about your relationship with God? As you contemplate the nature of that relationship, here are a few things to consider:

1. You will have a relationship with God; the only question is the nature of that relationship. The burning question is whether that relationship will be one that seeks to place Him first, or one that attempts to relegate Him to a position of lesser importance.

2. Your relationship with the Creator is ongoing; it unfolds day by day, and it offers countless opportunities to grow closer to Him . . . or not. As each new day unfolds, you are confronted with a wide range of decisions: how you will behave, where you will direct your thoughts, with whom you will associate, and what you will choose to worship. These choices, along with many others, are yours and yours alone. How you choose determines how your relationship with God will unfold.

3. God doesn't call you to be a run-of-the-mill, luke-warm believer. He invites you to form a radical, life-

changing relationship with Him. When you accept God's invitation--when you allow His Son to transform your life now and forever—you will become a different woman.

4. Once you decide to follow Christ completely and without reservation, you will gain the courage to change your life for the better as you follow in His footsteps and do the work of His kingdom.

5. Your decision to seek a deeper relationship with Christ will not remove all problems from your life. To the contrary, it will bring about a series of personal crises as you constantly seek to say "yes" to God although the world encourages you to do otherwise. Your responsibility—a responsibility that you must take very seriously--is to follow Christ and serve Him faithfully, even when you're tempted to give in or give up.

During the next 100 days, you'll be challenged to place God first in your life. And, you will be encouraged to place others second. Finally, you will be asked to examine yourself: your habits, your relationships, and your spiritual health.

As you consider the ideas in this text, remember that every day provides opportunities to put God where He belongs: at the center of your life. When you do so, you'll experience radical change and personal transformation as you worship Him, not just with words, but with deeds. This book is intended to remind you of the eternal promises that are found in God's Holy Word and of God's never-ending love for You. May these pages be a blessing to you, and may you, in turn, be a blessing to those whom God has seen fit to place along your path.

DAY 1

PUTTING GOD FIRST

But seek first the kingdom of God and His righteousness, and all these things will be provided for you.

Matthew 6:33 HCSB

The best way to radically change your life—and the surest way—is to do it with God as your partner. So here's a question worth thinking about: Have you made God a full partner in your life's journey? Or are you in the habit of giving God little more than a few hours on Sunday morning? The answer to this question will determine, to a surprising degree, the direction of your day and the quality of your life.

As you contemplate your own relationship with the Creator, remember this: Everybody, without exception, is engaged in the practice of worship. Some folks choose to worship God and, as a result, reap the rewards that He has promised. Other folks, folks who seem determined to do it "their way," inadvertently distance themselves from God, and from the path He intends for them to follow . . . and when they do, they suffer.

In the book of Exodus, God warns that we should place no gods before Him. Yet all too often, we place Him in second, third, or fourth place as we allow ourselves to be sidetracked by the temptations, addictions, and distractions that are woven into the fabric of 21st-century life.

Are you working to keep God first in your life? Do you talk with Him seven days a week, not just on Sunday mornings? And do you make big decisions after you've consulted Him, not before? Make certain that the honest answer to all of these questions is a resounding yes. Today and every day, put God first. No exceptions.

> Love has its source in God,
> for love is the very essence of His being.
>
> Kay Arthur

Jesus Christ is the first and last, author and finisher, beginning and end, alpha and omega, and by Him all other things hold together. He must be first or nothing. God never comes next!

Vance Havner

If God has the power to create and sustain the universe, He is more than able to sustain your marriage and your ministry, your faith and your finances, your hope and your health.

Anne Graham Lotz

It is when we come to the Lord in our nothingness, our powerlessness and our helplessness that He then enables us to love in a way which, without Him, would be absolutely impossible.

Elisabeth Elliot

When all else is gone, God is still left. Nothing changes Him.

Hannah Whitall Smith

GOD FIRST...OTHERS SECOND...

You must guard your heart by putting God in His rightful place—first place.

DAY 2

PUTTING THE NEEDS OF OTHERS AHEAD OF YOUR OWN

Be strong and of good courage, and do it; do not fear nor be dismayed, for the Lord God—my God—will be with you. He will not leave you nor forsake you, until you have finished all the work for the service of the house of the Lord.

1 Chronicles 28:20 NKJV

Jesus teaches that the most esteemed men and women are not the self-congratulatory leaders of society but are instead the humblest of servants. But, as weak human beings, we sometimes fall short as we seek to puff ourselves up and glorify our own accomplishments. To do so is wrong.

Today, you may feel the temptation to build yourself up in the eyes of your neighbors. Resist that temptation. Instead, serve your neighbors quietly and without fanfare. Find a need and fill it . . . humbly. Lend a helping hand and share a word of kindness…anonymously. This is God's way.

As a humble servant, you will glorify yourself, not before men, but before God, and that's what God intends. After all, earthly glory is fleeting: here today and all too soon gone. But, heavenly glory endures throughout eternity. So, the choice is yours: Either you can lift yourself up here on earth and be humbled in heaven, or vice versa. Choose vice versa.

God wants us to serve Him with a willing spirit, one that would choose no other way.

Beth Moore

In the very place where God has put us, whatever its limitations, whatever kind of work it may be, we may indeed serve the Lord Christ.

Elisabeth Elliot

Through our service to others, God wants to influence our world for Him.

Vonette Bright

If you want to discover your spiritual gifts, start obeying God. As you serve Him, you will find that He has given you the gifts that are necessary to follow through in obedience.

Anne Graham Lotz

GOD FIRST...OTHERS SECOND...

The direction of your steps and the quality of your life will be determined by the level of your service.

DAY 3

YOUR SPIRITUAL JOURNEY

Like newborn infants, desire the unadulterated spiritual milk, so that you may grow by it in your salvation.

1 Peter 2:2 HCSB

When will you be a "fully-grown" Christian woman? Hopefully never—or at least not until you arrive in heaven! As a believer living here on planet earth, you're never "fully grown"; you always have the potential to keep growing.

In those quiet moments when you open your heart to God, the One who made you keeps remaking you. He gives you direction, perspective, wisdom, and courage.

Would you like a time-tested formula for spiritual growth? Here it is: keep studying God's Word, keep obeying His commandments, keep praying (and listening for answers), and keep trying to live in the center of God's will. When you do, you'll never stay stuck for long. You will, instead, be a growing Christian . . . and that's precisely the kind of Christian God wants you to be.

If you want to discover your spiritual gifts, start obeying God. As you serve Him, you will find that He has given you the gifts that are necessary to follow through in obedience.

Anne Graham Lotz

We set our eyes on the finish line, forgetting the past, and straining toward the mark of spiritual maturity and fruitfulness.

Vonette Bright

A spiritual gift is a manifestation of God at work through you. God works in and through you to bear fruit. The focus is on God and what He does through you.

Henry Blackaby and Claude King

You are either becoming more like Christ every day or you're becoming less like Him. There is no neutral position in the Lord.

Stormie Omartian

GOD FIRST...OTHERS SECOND...

One way to guard your heart is by continuing to grow in your faith.

DAY 4

KEEP SEARCHING FOR WISDOM

Now if any of you lacks wisdom, he should ask God, who gives to all generously and without criticizing, and it will be given to him. But let him ask in faith without doubting. For the doubter is like the surging sea, driven and tossed by the wind.

James 1:5-6 HCSB

Where will you find wisdom today? Will you seek it from God or from the world? As a thoughtful woman living in a society that is filled with temptations and distractions, you know that the world's brand of "wisdom" is everywhere . . . and it is dangerous. You live in a world where it's all too easy to stray far from the ultimate source of wisdom: God's Holy Word.

When you commit yourself to the daily study of God's Word—and when you live according to His commandments—you will become wise . . . in time. But don't expect to open your Bible today and be wise tomorrow. Wisdom is not like a mushroom; it does not spring up overnight. It is, instead, like a majestic oak tree that starts as a tiny acorn, grows into a sapling, and eventually reaches up to the sky, tall and strong.

Today and every day, as a way of understanding God's plan for your life, you should study His Word and live by it.

When you do, you will accumulate a storehouse of wisdom that will enrich your own life and the lives of your family members, your friends, and the world.

This is my song through endless ages:
Jesus led me all the way.

Fanny Crosby

WOMEN

If we neglect the Bible, we cannot expect to benefit from the wisdom and direction that result from knowing God's Word.

Vonette Bright

Knowledge can be found in books or in school. Wisdom, on the other hand, starts with God . . . and ends there.

Marie T. Freeman

Wisdom is knowledge applied. Head knowledge is useless on the battlefield. Knowledge stamped on the heart makes one wise.

Beth Moore

When you and I are related to Jesus Christ, our strength and wisdom and peace and joy and love and hope may run out, but His life rushes in to keep us filled to the brim. We are showered with blessings, not because of anything we have or have not done, but simply because of Him.

Anne Graham Lotz

GOD FIRST...OTHERS SECOND...

God makes His wisdom available to you. Your job is to acknowledge, to understand, and (above all) to use that wisdom.

DAY 5

WANT RADICAL CHANGES? PRAY FOR THEM!

Rejoice in hope; be patient in affliction; be persistent in prayer.

Romans 12:12 HCSB

On his second missionary journey, Paul started a small church in Thessalonica. A short time later, he penned a letter that was intended to encourage the new believers at that church. Today, almost 2,000 years later, 1 Thessalonians remains a powerful, practical guide for Christian living.

In his letter, Paul advised members of the new church to "pray without ceasing." His advice applies to Christians of every generation. When we consult God on an hourly basis, we avail ourselves of His wisdom, His strength, and His love. As Corrie ten Boom observed, "Any concern that is too small to be turned into a prayer is too small to be made into a burden."

Today, instead of turning things over in your mind, turn them over to God in prayer. Instead of worrying about your next decision, ask God to lead the way. Don't limit your prayers to meals or bedtime. Become a woman of constant prayer. God is listening, and He wants to hear from you. Now.

Repentance removes old sins and wrong attitudes, and it opens the way for the Holy Spirit to restore our spiritual health.

Shirley Dobson

God gives us permission to forget our past and the understanding to live our present. He said He will remember our sins no more. (Psalm 103:11-12)

Serita Ann Jakes

When we reach the end of our strength, wisdom, and personal resources, we enter into the beginning of his glorious provisions.

Patsy Clairmont

In those desperate times when we feel like we don't have an ounce of strength, He will gently pick up our heads so that our eyes can behold something—something that will keep His hope alive in us.

Kathy Troccoli

GOD FIRST...OTHERS SECOND...

Prayer changes things and it changes you. So pray.

DAY 6

LETTING GOD'S WORD
LIGHT YOUR PATH

Your word is a lamp to my feet and a light to my path.

Psalm 119:105 NKJV

The Psalmist describes God's Word as, "a lamp to my feet." Is the Bible your lamp, too? If not, you are depriving yourself of a priceless gift from the Creator. Vance Havner observed, "It takes calm, thoughtful, prayerful meditation on the Word to extract its deepest nourishment." And make no mistake: you need that kind of nourishment.

Are you a woman who trusts God's Word without reservation? Hopefully so, because the Bible is unlike any other book—it is a guidebook for life here on earth and for life eternal.

God's Word can be a light to guide your steps. Claim it as your light today, tomorrow, and every day of your life—and then walk confidently in the footsteps of God's only begotten Son.

WOMEN

The Bible is God's Word to man.

Kay Arthur

Weave the unveiling fabric of God's word through your heart and mind. It will hold strong, even if the rest of life unravels.

Gigi Graham Tchividjian

I need the spiritual revival that comes from spending quiet time alone with Jesus in prayer and in thoughtful meditation on His Word.

Anne Graham Lotz

God can see clearly no matter how dark or foggy the night is. Trust His Word to guide you safely home.

Lisa Whelchel

Words fail to express my love for this holy Book, my gratitude for its author, for His love and goodness. How shall I thank him for it?

Lottie Moon

GOD FIRST...OTHERS SECOND...

On your bookshelf you have God's roadmap for daily life and for life eternal. How you choose to use your Bible is, of course, up to you . . . and so are the consequences.

DAY 7

FIRST THINGS FIRST

Therefore, get your minds ready for action, being self-disciplined . . . .

1 Peter 1:13 HCSB

"First things first." These words are easy to speak but hard to put into practice. For busy women living in a demanding world, placing first things first can be difficult indeed. Why? Because so many people are expecting so many things from us!

If you're having trouble prioritizing your day, perhaps you've been trying to organize your life according to your own plans, not God's. A better strategy, of course, is to take your daily obligations and place them in the hands of the One who created you. To do so, you must prioritize your day according to God's commandments, and you must seek His will and His wisdom in all matters. Then, you can face the day with the assurance that the same God who created our universe out of nothingness will help you place first things first in your own life.

Do you feel overwhelmed or confused? Turn the concerns of this day over to God—prayerfully, earnestly, and often. Then listen for His answer . . . and trust the answer He gives.

Have you prayed about your resources lately? Find out how God wants you to use your time and your money. No matter what it costs, forsake all that is not of God.

Kay Arthur

There were endless demands on Jesus' time. Still he was able to make that amazing claim of "completing the work you gave me to do." (John 17:4 NIV)

Elisabeth Elliot

Sin is largely a matter of mistaken priorities. Any sin in us that is cherished, hidden, and not confessed will cut the nerve center of our faith.

Catherine Marshall

The moment you wake up each morning, all your wishes and hopes for the day rush at you like wild animals. And the first job each morning consists in shoving it all back; in listening to that other voice, taking that other point of view, letting that other, larger, stronger, quieter life coming flowing in.

C. S. Lewis

Let's face it. None of us can do a thousand things to the glory of God. And, in our own vain attempt to do so, we stand the risk of forfeiting a precious thing.

Beth Moore

GOD FIRST...OTHERS SECOND...

Your Heavenly Father wants you to prioritize your day and your life. And the best place to start is by putting God first.

DAY 8

MAKING GOD'S PRIORITIES YOUR PRIORITIES

Draw near to God, and He will draw near to you.

James 4:8 HCSB

Have you fervently asked God to help prioritize your life? Have you asked Him for guidance and for the courage to do the things that you know need to be done? If so, then you're continually inviting your Creator to reveal Himself in a variety of ways. As a follower of Christ, you must do no less.

When you make God's priorities your priorities, you will receive God's abundance and His peace. When you make God a full partner in every aspect of your life, He will lead you along the proper path: His path. When you allow God to reign over your heart, He will honor you with spiritual blessings that are simply too numerous to count. So, as you plan for the day ahead, make God's will your ultimate priority. When you do, every other priority will have a tendency to fall neatly into place.

How important it is for us—young and old—to live as if Jesus would return any day—to set our goals, make our choices, raise our children, and conduct business with the perspective of the imminent return of our Lord.

Gloria Gaither

Whatever you love most, be it sports, pleasure, business or God, that is your god.

Billy Graham

Blessed are those who know what on earth they are here on earth to do and set themselves about the business of doing it.

Max Lucado

The essence of the Christian life is Jesus: that in all things He might have the preeminence, not that in some things He might have a place.

Franklin Graham

GOD FIRST...OTHERS SECOND...

The priorities you choose will dictate the life you live. So choose carefully.

DAY 9

THE GOOD NEWS

Grace to you and peace from God our Father and the Lord Jesus Christ.

Philippians 1:2 HCSB

God's grace is not earned . . . thank goodness! To earn God's love and His gift of eternal life would be far beyond the abilities of even the most righteous man or woman. Thankfully, grace is not an earthly reward for righteous behavior; it is a blessed spiritual gift which can be accepted by believers who dedicate themselves to God through Christ. When we accept Christ into our hearts, we are saved by His grace.

The familiar words of Ephesians 2:8 make God's promise perfectly clear: It is by grace we have been saved, through faith. We are saved not because of our good deeds but because of our faith in Christ.

God's grace is the ultimate gift, and we owe to Him the ultimate in thanksgiving. Let us praise the Creator for His priceless gift, and let us share the Good News with all who cross our paths. We return our Father's love by accepting His grace and by sharing His message and His love. When we do, we are eternally blessed . . . and the Father smiles.

God does what few men can do—forgets the sins of others.

Anonymous

Forgiveness is God's command.

Martin Luther

God forgets the past. Imitate him.

Max Lucado

I believe that forgiveness can become a continuing cycle: because God forgives us, we're to forgive others; because we forgive others, God forgives us. Scripture presents both parts of the cycle.

Shirley Dobson

When God forgives, He forgets. He buries our sins in the sea and puts a sign on the shore saying, "No Fishing Allowed."

Corrie ten Boom

GOD FIRST...OTHERS SECOND...

God's grace isn't earned, but freely given—what an amazing, humbling gift.

DAY 10

ENTRUSTING YOUR HOPES
TO GOD

You, Lord, give true peace to those who depend on you, because they trust you.

Isaiah 26:3 NCV

As every woman knows, hope is a perishable commodity. Despite God's promises, despite Christ's love, and despite our countless blessings, we frail human beings can still lose hope from time to time. When we do, we need the encouragement of Christian friends, the life-changing power of prayer, and the healing truth of God's Holy Word. If we find ourselves falling into the spiritual traps of worry and discouragement, we should seek the healing touch of Jesus and the encouraging words of fellow Christians. Even though this world can be a place of trials and struggles, God has promised us peace, joy, and eternal life if we give ourselves to Him.

Never yield to gloomy anticipation. Place your hope and confidence in God. He has no record of failure.

Mrs. Charles E. Cowman

The best we can hope for in this life is a knothole peek at the shining realities ahead. Yet a glimpse is enough. It's enough to convince our hearts that whatever sufferings and sorrows currently assail us aren't worthy of comparison to that which waits over the horizon.

Joni Eareckson Tada

Love is the seed of all hope. It is the enticement to trust, to risk, to try, and to go on.

Gloria Gaither

Easter comes each year to remind us of a truth that is eternal and universal. The empty tomb of Easter morning says to you and me, "Of course you'll encounter trouble. But behold a God of power who can take any evil and turn it into a door of hope."

Catherine Marshall

GOD FIRST...OTHERS SECOND...

Since God has promised to guide and protect you—now and forever—you should never lose hope.

DAY 11

VERY BIG PLANS

Teach me to do Your will, for You are my God. May Your gracious Spirit lead me on level ground.

Psalm 143:10 HCSB

God has plans for your life, but He won't force His plans upon you. Your Creator has given you the ability to make decisions on your own. With that freedom comes the responsibility of living with the consequences of your choices.

If you seek to live in accordance with God's plan for your life, you will study His Word, you will be attentive to His instructions, and you will be watchful for His signs. You will associate with fellow believers who, by their words and actions, will encourage your own spiritual growth. You will assiduously avoid those two terrible temptations: the temptation to sin and the temptation to squander time. And finally, you will listen carefully, even reverently, to the conscience that God has placed in your heart.

God has glorious plans for your day and your life. So as you go about your daily activities, keep your eyes and ears open . . . as well as your heart.

God has plans—not problems—for our lives. Before she died in the concentration camp in Ravensbruck, my sister Betsie said to me, "Corrie, your whole life has been a training for the work you are doing here in prison—and for the work you will do afterward."

Corrie ten Boom

Let's never forget that some of God's greatest mercies are His refusals. He says no in order that He may, in some way we cannot imagine, say yes. All His ways with us are merciful. His meaning is always love.

Elisabeth Elliot

God cannot lead the individual who is not willing to give Him a blank check with his life.

Catherine Marshall

Our souls were made to live in an upper atmosphere, and we stifle and choke if we live on any lower level. Our eyes were made to look off from these heavenly heights, and our vision is distorted by any lower gazing.

Hannah Whitall Smith

GOD FIRST...OTHERS SECOND...

God has a plan for your life. Your job is to discover that plan and follow it.

DAY 12

LETTING GOD TRANSFORM YOUR LIFE

Your old life is dead. Your new life, which is your real life—even though invisible to spectators—is with Christ in God. He is your life.

Think, for a moment, about the "old" you, the person you were before you invited Christ to reign over your heart. Now, think about the "new" you, the person you have become since then. Is there a difference between the "old" you and the "new and improved" version? There should be! And that difference should be noticeable not only to you but also to others.

The Bible clearly teaches that when we welcome Christ into our hearts, we become new creations through Him. Our challenge, of course, is to behave ourselves like new creations. When we do, God fills our hearts, He blesses our endeavors, and transforms our lives . . . forever.

If you are God's child, you are no longer bound to your past or to what you were. You are a brand new creature in Christ Jesus.

Kay Arthur

There is so much Heaven around us now if we have eyes for it, because eternity starts when we give ourselves to God.

Gloria Gaither

Repentance involves a radical change of heart and mind in which we agree with God's evaluation of our sin and then take specific action to align ourselves with His will.

Henry Blackaby

If we accept His invitation to salvation, we live with Him forever. However, if we do not accept because we refuse His only Son as our Savior, then we exclude ourselves from My Father's House. It's our choice.

Anne Graham Lotz

GOD FIRST...OTHERS SECOND...

Unless you're a radically different person because of your relationship with Jesus, your faith isn't what it could be . . . or should be.

DAY 13

CHOOSING TO PERSEVERE

But thanks be to God, who gives us the victory through our Lord Jesus Christ. Therefore, my beloved brethren, be steadfast, immovable, always abounding in the work of the Lord, knowing that your labor is not in vain in the Lord.

1 Corinthians 15:57–58 NKJV

A well-lived life is like a marathon, not a sprint—it calls for preparation, determination, and, of course, lots of perseverance. As an example of perfect perseverance, we Christians need look no further than our Savior, Jesus Christ.

Jesus finished what He began. Despite His suffering and despite the shame of the cross, Jesus was steadfast in His faithfulness to God. We, too, must remain faithful, especially during times of hardship. Sometimes, God may answer our prayers with silence, and when He does, we must patiently persevere.

Are you facing a tough situation? If so, remember this: whatever your problem, God can handle it. Your job is to keep persevering until He does.

Your life is not a boring stretch of highway. It's a straight line to heaven. And just look at the fields ripening along the way. Look at the tenacity and endurance. Look at the grains of righteousness. You'll have quite a crop at harvest...so don't give up!

Joni Eareckson Tada

Failure is one of life's most powerful teachers. How we handle our failures determines whether we're going to simply "get by" in life or "press on."

Beth Moore

If things are tough, remember that every flower that ever bloomed had to go through a whole lot of dirt to get there.

Barbara Johnson

Instead of being frustrated and overwhelmed by all that is going on in our world, go to the Lord and ask Him to give you His eternal perspective.

Kay Arthur

GOD FIRST...OTHERS SECOND...

Life is an exercise in perseverance. If you persevere, you win.

God never gives up
on you,
so don't you ever
give up on Him.

Marie T. Freeman

DAY 14

HE'S RIGHT HERE, RIGHT NOW

The Lord is with you when you are with Him. If you seek Him, He will be found by you.

2 Chronicles 15:2 HCSB

Since God is everywhere, we are free to sense His presence whenever we take the time to quiet our souls and turn our prayers to Him. But sometimes, amid the incessant demands of everyday life, we turn our thoughts far from God; when we do, we suffer.

Do you set aside quiet moments each day to offer praise to your Creator? As a woman who has received the gift of God's grace, you most certainly should. Silence is a gift that you give to yourself and to God. During these moments of stillness, you will often sense the infinite love and power of your Creator—and He, in turn, will speak directly to your heart.

The familiar words of Psalm 46:10 remind us to "Be still, and know that I am God." When we do so, we encounter the awesome presence of our loving Heavenly Father, and we are comforted in the knowledge that God is not just near. He is here.

WOMEN

It's a crazy world and life speeds by at a blur, yet God is right in the middle of the craziness. And anywhere, at anytime, we may turn to Him, hear His voice, feel His hand, and catch the fragrance of heaven.

Joni Eareckson Tada

In the sanctuary, we discover beauty: the beauty of His presence.

Kay Arthur

Our souls were made to live in an upper atmosphere, and we stifle and choke if we live on any lower level. Our eyes were made to look off from these heavenly heights, and our vision is distorted by any lower gazing.

Hannah Whitall Smith

Through the death and broken body of Jesus Christ on the Cross, you and I have been given access to the presence of God when we approach Him by faith in prayer.

Anne Graham Lotz

GOD FIRST...OTHERS SECOND...

God isn't far away—He's right here, right now. And He's willing to talk to you right here, right now.

DAY 15

FOLLOWING YOUR CONSCIENCE

Let us draw near with a true heart in full assurance of faith, our hearts sprinkled clean from an evil conscience and our bodies washed in pure water.

Hebrews 10:22 HCSB

God gave you a conscience for a very good reason: to make your path conform to His will. Billy Graham correctly observed, "Most of us follow our conscience as we follow a wheelbarrow. We push it in front of us in the direction we want to go." To do so, of course, is a profound mistake. Yet all of us, on occasion, have failed to listen to the voice that God planted in our hearts, and all of us have suffered the consequences.

Wise believers make it a practice to listen carefully to that quiet internal voice. Count yourself among that number. When your conscience speaks, listen and learn. In all likelihood, God is trying to get His message through. And in all likelihood, it is a message that you desperately need to hear.

WOMEN

God desires that we become spiritually healthy enough through faith to have a conscience that rightly interprets the work of the Holy Spirit.

Beth Moore

If I am walking along the street with a very disfiguring hole in the back of my dress, of which I am in ignorance, it is certainly a very great comfort to me to have a kind friend who will tell me of it. And similarly, it is indeed a comfort to know that there is always abiding with me a divine, all-seeing Comforter, who will reprove me for all my faults and will not let me go on in a fatal unconsciousness of them.

Hannah Whitall Smith

My conscience is captive to the word of God.

Martin Luther

Your conscience is your alarm system. It's your protection.

Charles Stanley

GOD FIRST...OTHERS SECOND...

If your friends are telling you one thing and your conscience is telling you something else, trust your conscience.

DAY 16

TOO MANY DISTRACTIONS?

Keep your eyes on Jesus, who both began and finished this race we're in. Study how he did it. Because he never lost sight of where he was headed, that exhilarating finish in and with God, he could put up with anything along the way: cross, shame, whatever. And now he's there, in the place of honor, right alongside God.

Hebrews 12:2 MSG

All of us must live through those days when the traffic jams, the computer crashes, and the dog makes a main course out of our homework. But, when we find ourselves distracted by the minor frustrations of life, we must catch ourselves, take a deep breath, and lift our thoughts upward.

Although we may, at times, struggle mightily to rise above the distractions of everyday living, we need never struggle alone. God is here—eternal and faithful, with infinite patience and love—and, if we reach out to Him, He will restore our sense of perspective and give peace to our souls.

Give me the person
who says,
"This one thing I do,
and not these fifty
things I dabble in."

D. L. Moody

Among the enemies to devotion, none is so harmful as distractions. Whatever excites the curiosity, scatters the thoughts, disquiets the heart, absorbs the interests, or shifts our life focus from the kingdom of God within us to the world around us—that is a distraction; and the world is full of them.

A. W. Tozer

The demand of every day kept me so busy that I subconsciously equated my busyness with commitment to Christ.

Vonette Bright

You can't get second things by putting them first; you can get second things only by putting first things first.

C. S. Lewis

We need to stop focusing on our lacks and stop giving out excuses and start looking at and listening to Jesus.

Anne Graham Lotz

GOD FIRST...OTHERS SECOND...

With all the distractions in the world, let Jesus be your main attraction.

DAY 17

TO RADICALLY CHANGE YOUR DAY, TALK TO GOD EVERY MORNING

But have nothing to do with irreverent and silly myths. Rather, train yourself in godliness.

1 Timothy 4:7 HCSB

Each new day is a gift from God, and if we are wise, we spend a few quiet moments each morning thanking the Giver. Daily life is woven together with the threads of habit, and no habit is more important to our spiritual health than the discipline of daily prayer and devotion to the Creator.

When we begin each day with heads bowed and hearts lifted, we remind ourselves of God's love, His protection, and His commandments. And if we are wise, we align our priorities for the coming day with the teachings and commandments that God has given us through His Holy Word.

Are you seeking to change some aspect of your life? Do you seek to improve the condition of your spiritual or physical health? If so, ask for God's help and ask for it many times each day—starting with your morning devotional.

Jesus challenges you and me to keep our focus daily on the cross of His will if we want to be His disciples.

Anne Graham Lotz

I suggest you discipline yourself to spend time daily in a systematic reading of God's Word. Make this "quiet time" a priority that nobody can change.

Warren Wiersbe

A person with no devotional life generally struggles with faith and obedience.

Charles Stanley

Knowing God involves an intimate, personal relationship that is developed over time through prayer and getting answers to prayer, through Bible study and applying its teaching to our lives, through obedience and experiencing the power of God, through moment-by-moment submission to Him that results in a moment-by-moment filling of the Holy Spirit.

Anne Graham Lotz

GOD FIRST...OTHERS SECOND...

You need a regular appointment with your Creator. God is ready to talk to you, and you should prepare yourself each morning to talk to Him.

DAY 18

BE A JOYFUL CHRISTIAN

Make me hear joy and gladness.

Psalm 51:8 NKJV

Barbara Johnson says, "You have to look for the joy. Look for the light of God that is hitting your life, and you will find sparkles you didn't know were there."

Have you experienced that kind of joy? Hopefully so, because it's not enough to hear someone else talk about being joyful—you must actually experience that kind of joy in order to understand it.

Should you expect to be a joy-filled woman 24 hours a day, seven days a week, from this moment on? No. But you can (and should) experience pockets of joy frequently—that's the kind of joy-filled life that a woman like you deserves to live.

What is your focus today?
Joy comes when it is Jesus first,
others second...then you.

Kay Arthur

The Christian lifestyle is not one of legalistic do's and don'ts, but one that is positive, attractive, and joyful.

Vonette Bright

If you're a thinking Christian, you will be a joyful Christian.

Marie T. Freeman

There may be no trumpet sound or loud applause when we make a right decision, just a calm sense of resolution and peace.

Gloria Gaither

Jesus did not promise to change the circumstances around us. He promised great peace and pure joy to those who would learn to believe that God actually controls all things.

Corrie ten Boom

GOD FIRST...OTHERS SECOND...

Every day, God gives you cause to rejoice. And the rest is up to you.

DAY 19

NEW BEGINNINGS

Then the One seated on the throne said, "Look! I am making everything new."

Revelation 21:5 HCSB

Each new day offers countless opportunities to serve God, to seek His will, and to obey His teachings. But each day also offers countless opportunities to stray from God's commandments and to wander far from His path.

Sometimes, we wander aimlessly in a wilderness of our own making, but God has better plans for us. And, whenever we ask Him to renew our strength and guide our steps, He does so.

Consider this day a new beginning. Consider it a fresh start, a renewed opportunity to serve your Creator with willing hands and a loving heart. Ask God to renew your sense of purpose as He guides your steps. Today is a glorious opportunity to serve God. Seize that opportunity while you can; tomorrow may indeed be too late.

God is not running an antique shop! He is making all things new!

The amazing thing about Jesus is that He doesn't just patch up our lives, He gives us a brand new sheet, a clean slate to start over, all new.

Gloria Gaither

Like a spring of pure water, God's peace in our hearts brings cleansing and refreshment to our minds and bodies.

Billy Graham

Whoever you are, whatever your condition or circumstance, whatever your past or problem, Jesus can restore you to wholeness.

Anne Graham Lotz

GOD FIRST...OTHERS SECOND...

If you're graduating into a new phase of life, be sure to make God your partner. If you do, He'll guide your steps, He'll help carry your burdens, and He'll help you focus on the things that really matter.

DAY 20

SEEK FELLOWSHIP

Then all the people began to eat and drink, send portions, and have a great celebration, because they had understood the words that were explained to them.

Nehemiah 8:12 HCSB

Fellowship with other believers should be an integral part of your everyday life. Your association with fellow Christians should be uplifting, enlightening, encouraging, and consistent.

Are you an active member of your own fellowship? Are you a builder of bridges inside the four walls of your church and outside it? Do you contribute to God's glory by contributing your time and your talents to a close-knit band of believers? Hopefully so. The fellowship of believers is intended to be a powerful tool for spreading God's Good News and uplifting His children. And God intends for you to be a fully contributing member of that fellowship. Your intentions should be the same.

Be united with other Christians. A wall with loose bricks is not good. The bricks must be cemented together.

Corrie ten Boom

One of the ways God refills us after failure is through the blessing of Christian fellowship. Just experiencing the joy of simple activities shared with other children of God can have a healing effect on us.

Anne Graham Lotz

In God's economy you will be hard-pressed to find many examples of successful "Lone Rangers."

Luci Swindoll

Christians are like coals of a fire. Together they glow—apart they grow cold.

Anonymous

When many men rejoice together, there is a richer job in each individual, since they enkindle themselves and they inflame one another.

St. Augustine

GOD FIRST...OTHERS SECOND...

You need fellowship with men and women of faith. And your Christian friends need fellowship with you. So what are you waiting for?

DAY 21

FORGIVE EVERYBODY

For if you forgive people their wrongdoing, your Heavenly Father will forgive you as well. But if you don't forgive people, your Father will not forgive your wrongdoing.

Matthew 6:14-15 HCSB

The world holds few if any rewards for those who remain angrily focused upon the past. Still, the act of forgiveness is difficult for all but the most saintly men and women. Are you mired in the quicksand of bitterness or regret? If so, you are not only disobeying God's Word, you are also wasting your time.

Being frail, fallible, imperfect human beings, most of us are quick to anger, quick to blame, slow to forgive, and even slower to forget. Yet as Christians, we are commanded to forgive others, just as we, too, have been forgiven.

If there exists even one person—alive or dead—against whom you hold bitter feelings, it's time to forgive. Or, if you are embittered against yourself for some past mistake or shortcoming, it's finally time to forgive yourself and move on. Hatred, bitterness, and regret are not part of God's plan for your life. Forgiveness is.

When God forgives, He forgets. He buries our sins in the sea and puts a sign on the shore saying, "No Fishing Allowed."

Corrie ten Boom

God expects us to forgive others as He has forgiven us; we are to follow His example by having a forgiving heart.

Vonette Bright

The more you practice the art of forgiving, the quicker you'll master the art of living.

Marie T. Freeman

Forgiveness is the precondition of love.

Catherine Marshall

GOD FIRST...OTHERS SECOND...

Forgiveness is its own reward. Bitterness is its own punishment. Guard your words and your thoughts accordingly.

DAY 22

LISTENING TO GOD

The one who is from God listens to God's words. This is why you don't listen, because you are not from God.

John 8:47 HCSB

Sometimes God speaks loudly and clearly. More often, He speaks in a quiet voice—and if you are wise, you will be listening carefully when He does. To do so, you must carve out quiet moments each day to study His Word and sense His direction.

Can you quiet yourself long enough to listen to your conscience? Are you attuned to the subtle guidance of your intuition? Are you willing to pray sincerely and then to wait quietly for God's response? Hopefully so. Usually God refrains from sending His messages on stone tablets or city billboards. More often, He communicates in subtler ways. If you sincerely desire to hear His voice, you must listen carefully, and you must do so in the silent corners of your quiet, willing heart.

When we come to Jesus stripped of pretensions, with a needy spirit, ready to listen, He meets us at the point of need.

Catherine Marshall

In the soul-searching of our lives, we are to stay quiet so we can hear Him say all that He wants to say to us in our hearts.

Charles Swindoll

The first service one owes to others in the fellowship consists in listening to them. Just as love of God begins in listening to His Word, so the beginning of love for the brethren is learning to listen to them.

Dietrich Bonhoeffer

We must leave it to God to answer our prayers in His own wisest way. Sometimes, we are so impatient and think that God does not answer. God always answers! He never fails! Be still. Abide in Him.

Mrs. Charles E. Cowman

GOD FIRST...OTHERS SECOND...

God is trying to get your attention. Are you listening?

DAY 23

CHOOSING TO CONTROL YOUR TEMPER

Don't let the sun go down on your anger, and don't give the Devil an opportunity.

Ephesians 4:26-27 HCSB

Sometimes, anger is appropriate. Even Jesus became angry when confronted with the moneychangers in the temple. On occasion, you, like Jesus, will confront evil, and when you do, you may respond as He did: vigorously and without reservation. But, more often than not, your frustrations will be of the more mundane variety. As long as you live here on earth, you will face countless opportunities to lose your temper over small, relatively insignificant events: a traffic jam, a spilled cup of coffee, an inconsiderate comment, a broken promise. When you are tempted to lose your temper over the minor inconveniences of life, don't. Turn away from anger, hatred, bitterness, and regret. Turn instead to God.

Life is too short to spend it being angry, bored, or dull.

Barbara Johnson

When something robs you of your peace of mind, ask yourself if it is worth the energy you are expending on it. If not, then put it out of your mind in an act of discipline. Every time the thought of "it" returns, refuse it.

Kay Arthur

If your temper gets the best of you . . . then other people get to see the worst in you.

Marie T. Freeman

Anger unresolved will only bring you woe.

Kay Arthur

Anger breeds remorse in the heart, discord in the home, bitterness in the community, and confusion in the state.

Billy Graham

GOD FIRST...OTHERS SECOND...

Angry words are dangerous to your emotional and spiritual health, not to mention your relationships. So treat anger as an uninvited guest, and usher it away as quickly—and as quietly—as possible.

DAY 24

BEWARE!

The good obtain favor from the Lord, but He condemns a man who schemes.

Proverbs 12:2 HCSB

This world is God's creation, and it contains the wonderful fruits of His handiwork. But, the world also contains countless opportunities to stray from God's will. Temptations are everywhere, and the devil, it seems, never takes a day off. Our task, as believers, is to turn away from temptation and to place our lives squarely in the center of God's will.

In his letter to Jewish Christians, Peter offered a stern warning: "Your adversary, the devil, prowls around like a roaring lion, seeking someone to devour" (1 Peter 5:8 NASB). What was true in New Testament times is equally true in our own. Evil is indeed abroad in the world, and Satan continues to sow the seeds of destruction far and wide. As Christians, we must guard our hearts by earnestly wrapping ourselves in the protection of God's Holy Word. When we do, we are protected.

Light is stronger than darkness—darkness cannot "comprehend" or "overcome" it.

Anne Graham Lotz

Where God's ministers are most successful, there the powers of darkness marshal their forces for the conflict.

Lottie Moon

Don't condone what God condemns.

Anonymous

We are in a continual battle with the spiritual forces of evil, but we will triumph when we yield to God's leading and call on His powerful presence in prayer.

Shirley Dobson

We actually are, at present, creatures whose character must be, in some respects, a horror to God, as it is, when we really see it, a horror to ourselves. This I believe to be a fact: and I notice that the holier a man is, the more fully he is aware of that fact.

C. S. Lewis

GOD FIRST...OTHERS SECOND...

Evil exists, and it exists someplace not too far from you. You must guard your steps and your heart accordingly.

DAY 25

ANSWERING GOD'S CALL

I urge you now to live the life to which God called you.

Ephesians 4:1 NKJV

God is calling you to follow a specific path that He has chosen for your life. And it is vitally important that you heed that call. Otherwise, your talents and opportunities may go unused.

Have you already heard God's call? And are you pursuing it with vigor? If so, you're both fortunate and wise. But if you have not yet discovered what God intends for you to do with your life, keep searching and keep praying until you discover why the Creator put you here.

Remember: God has important work for you to do—work that no one else on earth can accomplish but you. The Creator has placed you in a particular location, amid particular people, with unique opportunities to serve. And He has given you all the tools you need to succeed. So listen for His voice, watch for His signs, and prepare yourself for the call that is sure to come.

If God has called you, do not spend time looking over your shoulder to see who is following you.

Corrie ten Boom

He treats us as sons, and all He asks in return is that we shall treat Him as a Father whom we can trust without anxiety. We must take the son's place of dependence and trust, and we must let Him keep the father's place of care and responsibility.

Hannah Whitall Smith

God never calls without enabling us. In other words, if he calls you to do something, he makes it possible for you to do it.

Luci Swindoll

There is wonderful freedom and joy in coming to recognize that the fun is in the becoming.

Gloria Gaither

GOD FIRST...OTHERS SECOND...

God has a plan for your life, a divine calling that you can either answer or ignore. How you choose to respond to God's calling will determine the direction you take and the contributions you make.

DAY 26

NO PROBLEMS ARE TOO BIG FOR GOD

Blessed be the God and Father of our Lord Jesus Christ, the Father of mercies and the God of all comfort. He comforts us in all our affliction, so that we may be able to comfort those who are in any kind of affliction, through the comfort we ourselves receive from God.

2 Corinthians 1:3-4 HCSB

The Bible promises this: tough times are temporary but God's love is not—God's love lasts forever. So what does that mean to you? Just this: From time to time, everybody faces tough times, and so will you. And when tough times arrive, God will always stand ready to protect you and heal you.

Psalm 147 promises, "He heals the brokenhearted" (v. 3, NIV), but Psalm 147 doesn't say that He heals them instantly. Usually, it takes time (and maybe even a little help from you) for God to fix things. So if you're facing tough times, face them with God by your side. If you find yourself in any kind of trouble, pray about it and ask God for help. And be patient. God will work things out, just as He has promised, but He will do it in His own way and in His own time.

Measure the size of the obstacles against the size of God.

Beth Moore

If we're going to stand up and make a difference for Christ while others lounge about, you can be sure we'll encounter hardships, obstacles, nuisances, hassles, and inconveniences—much more than the average couch potato. And we shouldn't be surprised. Such difficulty while serving Christ isn't necessarily suffering—it's status quo.

Joni Eareckson Tada

Adversity is always unexpected and unwelcomed. It is an intruder and a thief, and yet in the hands of God, adversity becomes the means through which His supernatural power is demonstrated.

Charles Stanley

When God allows extraordinary trials for His people, He prepares extraordinary comforts for them.

Corrie ten Boom

GOD FIRST...OTHERS SECOND...

When you experience tough times (and you will), a positive attitude makes a big difference in the way you tackle your problems.

DAY 27

THE TIME FOR ACTION
IS NOW

When you make a vow to God, don't delay fulfilling it, because He does not delight in fools. Fulfill what you vow.

Ecclesiastes 5:4 HCSB

The old saying is both familiar and true: actions speak louder than words. And as believers, we must beware: our actions should always give credence to the changes that Christ can make in the lives of those who walk with Him.

God calls upon each of us to act in accordance with His will and with respect for His commandments. If we are to be responsible believers, we must realize that it is never enough simply to hear the instructions of God; we must also live by them. And it is never enough to wait idly by while others do God's work here on earth; we, too, must act. Doing God's work is a responsibility that each of us must bear, and when we do, our loving Heavenly Father rewards our efforts with a bountiful harvest.

We spend our lives dreaming of the future, not realizing that a little of it slips away every day.

Barbara Johnson

A bird does not know it can fly before it uses its wings. We learn God's love in our hearts as soon as we act upon it.

Corrie Ten Boom

From the very moment one feels called to act is born the strength to bear whatever horror one will feel or see. In some inexplicable way, terror loses its overwhelming power when it becomes a task that must be faced.

Emmi Bonhoeffer

God has lots of folks who intend to go to work for him "some day." What He needs is more people who are willing to work for Him this day.

Marie T. Freeman

Logic will not change an emotion, but action will.

Zig Ziglar

GOD FIRST...OTHERS SECOND...

Because actions do speak louder than words, it's always a good time to let your actions speak for themselves.

DAY 28

BE A PRACTICAL CHRISTIAN

Pure and undefiled religion before our God and Father is this: to look after orphans and widows in their distress and to keep oneself unstained by the world.

James 1:27 HCSB

What is "real" Christianity? Think of it as an ongoing relationship—an all-encompassing relationship with God and with His Son Jesus. It is inevitable that your life must be lived in relationship to God. The question is not if you will have a relationship with Him; the burning question is whether that relationship will be one that seeks to honor Him or one that seeks to ignore Him.

We live in a world that discourages heartfelt devotion and obedience to God. Everywhere we turn, or so it seems, we are confronted by a mind-numbing assortment of distractions, temptations, obligations, and frustrations. Yet even on our busiest days, God beckons us to slow down and consult Him. When we do, we avail ourselves of the peace and abundance that only He can give.

Every Christian is to become a little Christ. The whole purpose of becoming a Christian is simply nothing else.

C. S. Lewis

The Christian lifestyle is not one of legalistic do's and don'ts, but one that is positive, attractive, and joyful.

Vonette Bright

As you walk by faith, you live a righteous life, for righteousness is always by faith.

Kay Arthur

This life of faith, then, consists in just this—being a child in the Father's house. Let the ways of childish confidence and freedom from care, which so please you and win your heart when you observe your own little ones, teach you what you should be in your attitude toward God.

Hannah Whitall Smith

Faith has to be exercised in the midst of ordinary, down-to-earth living.

Elisabeth Elliot

GOD FIRST...OTHERS SECOND...

The difference between theological dogma and faith with works is the difference between stagnant religion and joyful Christianity.

DAY 29

CONSIDERING THE CROSS

But God forbid that I should boast except in the cross of our Lord Jesus Christ, by whom the world has been crucified to me, and I to the world.

Galatians 6:14 NKJV

As we consider Christ's sacrifice on the cross, we should be profoundly humbled and profoundly grateful. And today, as we come to Christ in prayer, we should do so in a spirit of quiet, heartfelt devotion to the One who gave His life so that we might have life eternal.

He was the Son of God, but He wore a crown of thorns. He was the Savior of mankind, yet He was put to death on a roughhewn cross made of wood. He offered His healing touch to an unsaved world, and yet the same hands that had healed the sick and raised the dead were pierced with nails.

Christ humbled Himself on a cross—for you. He shed His blood—for you. He has offered to walk with you through this life and throughout all eternity. As you approach Him today in prayer, think about His sacrifice and His grace. And be humble.

Jesus came down from heaven, revealing exactly what God is like, offering eternal life and a personal relationship with God, on the condition of our rebirth—a rebirth made possible through His own death on the cross.

Anne Graham Lotz

God is my Heavenly Father. He loves me with an everlasting love. The proof of that is the Cross.

Elisabeth Elliot

The cross takes care of the past. The cross takes care of the flesh. The cross takes care of the world.

Kay Arthur

The heaviest end of the cross lies ever on His shoulders. If He bids us carry a burden, He carries it also.

C. H. Spurgeon

God proved his love on the cross. When Christ hung, and bled, and died it was God saying to the world—I love you.

Billy Graham

GOD FIRST...OTHERS SECOND...

The salvation that Jesus provided on the cross is free to us, but it cost Him so much. We must never take His sacrifice for granted.

DAY 30

DON'T BE ENVIOUS

Let us walk properly, as in the day, not in revelry and drunkenness, not in lewdness and lust, not in strife and envy.

Romans 13:13 NKJV

In a competitive, cut-throat world, it is easy to become envious of others' success. But it's wrong.

We know intuitively that envy is wrong, but because we are frail, imperfect human beings, we may find ourselves struggling with feelings of envy or resentment, or both. These feelings may be especially forceful when we see other people experience unusually good fortune.

Have you recently felt the pangs of envy creeping into your heart? If so, it's time to focus on the marvelous things that God has done for you and your family. And just as importantly, you must refrain from preoccupying yourself with the blessings that God has chosen to give others.

So here's a surefire formula for a happier, healthier life: Count your own blessings and let your neighbors count theirs. It's the godly way to live.

What God asks, does, or requires of others is not my business; it is His.

Kay Arthur

Too many Christians envy the sinners their pleasure and the saints their joy because they don't have either one.

Martin Luther

We might occasionally be able to change our circumstances, but only God can change our hearts.

Beth Moore

To love involves trusting the beloved beyond the evidence, even against much evidence. No man is our friend who believes in our good intentions only when they are proved. No man is our friend who will not be very slow to accept evidence against them. Such confidence, between one man and another, is in fact almost universally praised as a mortal beauty, not blamed as a logical error. And the suspicious man is blamed for a meanness of character, not admired for the excellence of his logic.

C. S. Lewis

GOD FIRST...OTHERS SECOND...

Envy is a sin, a sin that robs you of contentment and peace. So you must refuse to let feelings of envy invade your thoughts or your heart.

DAY 31

TRUST GOD'S PROMISES

For you need endurance, so that after you have done God's will, you may receive what was promised.

What do you expect from the day ahead? Are you expecting God to do wonderful things, or are you living beneath a cloud of apprehension and doubt? The familiar words of Psalm 118:24 remind us of a profound yet simple truth: "This is the day which the LORD hath made; we will rejoice and be glad in it" (KJV).

For Christian believers, every day begins and ends with God's Son and God's promises. When we accept Christ into our hearts, God promises us the opportunity for earthly peace and spiritual abundance. But more importantly, God promises us the priceless gift of eternal life.

As we face the inevitable challenges of life here on earth, we must arm ourselves with the promises of God's Holy Word. When we do, we can expect the best, not only for the day ahead, but also for all eternity.

God will never let you sink under your circumstances. He always provide a safety net and His love always encircles.

Barbara Johnson

Only believe, don't fear. Our Master, Jesus, always watches over us, and no matter what the persecution, Jesus will surely overcome it.

Lottie Moon

Our future may look fearfully intimidating, yet we can look up to the Engineer of the Universe, confident that nothing escapes His attention or slips out of the control of those strong hands.

Elisabeth Elliot

Worries carry responsibilities that belong to God, not to you. Worry does not enable us to escape evil; it makes us unfit to cope with it when it comes.

Corrie ten Boom

GOD FIRST...OTHERS SECOND...

God has made many promises to you, and He will keep every single one of them. Your job is to trust God's promises and live accordingly.

DAY 32

CHOOSING TO HAVE A HEALTHY FEAR OF GOD

Therefore, since we are receiving a kingdom that cannot be shaken, let us hold on to grace. By it, we may serve God acceptably, with reverence and awe.

Hebrews 12:28 HCSB

Are you a woman who possesses a healthy, fearful respect for God's power? Hopefully so. After all, God's Word teaches that the fear of the Lord is the beginning of knowledge (Proverbs 1:7).

When we fear the Creator—and when we honor Him by obeying His commandments—we receive God's approval and His blessings. But, when we ignore Him or disobey His commandments, we invite disastrous consequences.

God's hand shapes the universe, and it shapes our lives. God maintains absolute sovereignty over His creation, and His power is beyond comprehension. The fear of the Lord is, indeed, the beginning of knowledge. But thankfully, once we possess a healthy, reverent fear of God, we need never be fearful of anything else.

A healthy fear of God will do much to deter us from sin.

Charles Swindoll

It is not possible that mortal men should be thoroughly conscious of the divine presence without being filled with awe.

C. H. Spurgeon

The remarkable thing about fearing God is that when you fear God, you fear nothing else, whereas if you do not fear God, you fear everything else.

Oswald Chambers

When true believers are awed by the greatness of God and by the privilege of becoming His children, then they become sincerely motivated, effective evangelists.

Bill Hybels

I'm convinced that there is nothing that can happen to me in this life that is not precisely designed by a sovereign Lord to give me the opportunity to learn to know Him.

Elisabeth Elliot

GOD FIRST...OTHERS SECOND...

If you have a healthy fear of God, you're wise—if you don't, you're not.

DAY 33

WHEN YOU HAVE DOUBTS

Now if any of you lacks wisdom, he should ask God, who gives to all generously and without criticizing, and it will be given to him. But let him ask in faith without doubting. For the doubter is like the surging sea, driven and tossed by the wind.

James 1:5-6 HCSB

If you've never had any doubts about your faith, then you can stop reading this page now and skip to the next. But if you've ever been plagued by doubts about your faith or your God, keep reading.

Even some of the most faithful Christians are, at times, beset by occasional bouts of discouragement and doubt. But even when we feel far removed from God, God is never far removed from us. He is always with us, always willing to calm the storms of life—always willing to replace our doubts with comfort and assurance.

Whenever you're plagued by doubts, that's precisely the moment you should seek God's presence by genuinely seeking to establish a deeper, more meaningful relationship with His Son. Then you may rest assured that in time, God will calm your fears, answer your prayers, and restore your confidence.

We are most vulnerable to the piercing winds of doubt when we distance ourselves from the mission and fellowship to which Christ has called us.

Joni Eareckson Tada

Disobedience to His Word will cause you to doubt.

Anne Graham Lotz

Fear and doubt are conquered by a faith that rejoices. And faith can rejoice because the promises of God are as certain as God Himself.

Kay Arthur

The Holy Spirit is no skeptic, and the things he has written in our hearts are not doubts or opinions, but assertions— surer and more certain than sense or life itself.

Martin Luther

Doubting may temporarily disturb, but will not permanently destroy, your faith in Christ.

Charles Swindoll

GOD FIRST...OTHERS SECOND...

When you have fears or doubts, don't ignore them. Talk to family, to friends, and, most importantly, to God.

DAY 34

REMEMBER: YOU DON'T HAVE TO BE PERFECT

Those who wait for perfect weather will never plant seeds; those who look at every cloud will never harvest crops. Plant early in the morning, and work until evening, because you don't know if this or that will succeed. They might both do well.

Ecclesiastes 11:4, 6 NCV

Expectations, expectations, expectations! As a woman living in the 21st century, you know that demands can be high, and expectations even higher. The media delivers an endless stream of messages that tell you how to look, how to behave, how to eat, and how to dress. The media's expectations are impossible to meet—God's are not. God doesn't expect you to be perfect . . . and neither should you.

Remember: the expectations that really matter are God's expectations. Everything else takes a back seat. So do your best to please God, and don't worry too much about what other people think. And, when it comes to meeting the unrealistic expectations of a world gone nuts, forget about trying to be perfect—it's impossible.

God is so inconceivably good. He's not looking for perfection. He already saw it in Christ. He's looking for affection.

Beth Moore

The happiest people in the world are not those who have no problems, but the people who have learned to live with those things that are less than perfect.

James Dobson

The greatest destroyer of good works is the desire to do great works.

C. H. Spurgeon

We shall never come to the perfect man til we come to the perfect world.

Matthew Henry

What makes a Christian a Christian is not perfection but forgiveness.

Max Lucado

GOD FIRST...OTHERS SECOND...

Don't worry about being perfect—it's impossible. God doesn't want your perfection; He wants your heart.

DAY 35

GUARD YOUR HEART AND MIND

Finally, brethren, whatever things are true, whatever things are noble, whatever things are just, whatever things are pure, whatever things are lovely, whatever things are of good report, if there is any virtue and if there is anything praiseworthy— meditate on these things.

Philippians 4:8 NKJV

You are near and dear to God. He loves you more than you can imagine, and He wants the very best for you. And one more thing: God wants you to guard your heart.

Every day, you are faced with choices . . . more choices than you can count. You can do the right thing, or not. You can be prudent, or not. You can be kind, and generous, and obedient to God. Or not.

Today, the world will offer you countless opportunities to let down your guard and, by doing so, make needless mistakes that may injure you or your loved ones. So be watchful and obedient. Guard your heart by giving it to your Heavenly Father; it is safe with Him.

Becoming pure is a process of spiritual growth, and taking seriously the confession of sin during prayer time moves that process along, causing us to purge our life of practices that displease God.

Elizabeth George

Holiness has never been the driving force of the majority. It is, however, mandatory for anyone who wants to enter the kingdom.

Elisabeth Elliot

He doesn't need an abundance of words. He doesn't need a dissertation about your life. He just wants your attention. He wants your heart.

Kathy Troccoli

We look at our burdens and heavy loads, and we shrink from them. But, if we lift them and bind them about our hearts, they become wings, and on them we can rise and soar toward God.

Mrs. Charles E. Cowman

GOD FIRST...OTHERS SECOND...

You should do whatever it takes to guard your heart—and with God's help, you can do it!

DAY 36

THE POWER OF INTEGRITY

A good name is to be chosen over great wealth.

Proverbs 22:1 HCSB

Honesty is the best policy, but it is not always the easiest policy. Sometimes, the truth hurts, and sometimes, it's tough to be a man of integrity . . . tough, but essential.

Charles Swindoll correctly observed, "Nothing speaks louder or more powerfully than a life of integrity." Godly men agree.

Integrity is built slowly over a lifetime. It is the sum of every right decision and every honest word. It is forged on the anvil of honorable work and polished by the twin virtues of honesty and fairness. Integrity is a precious thing— difficult to build but easy to tear down. As believers in Christ, we must seek to live each day with discipline, honesty, and faith. When we do, integrity becomes a habit. And God smiles.

God never called us to naïveté. He called us to integrity....
The biblical concept of integrity emphasizes mature
innocence not childlike ignorance.

Beth Moore

Integrity is a sign of maturity.

Charles Swindoll

The single most important element in any human
relationship is honesty—with oneself, with God, and with
others.

Catherine Marshall

You cannot glorify Christ and practice deception at the
same time.

Warren Wiersbe

The commandment of absolute truthfulness is really only
another name for the fullness of discipleship.

Dietrich Bonhoeffer

GOD FIRST...OTHERS SECOND...

The real test of integrity is being willing to tell the truth
when it's hard.

DAY 37

RADICAL ENTHUSIASM

Don't work only while being watched, in order to please men, but as slaves of Christ, do God's will from your heart. Render service with a good attitude, as to the Lord and not to men.

Ephesians 6:6-7 HCSB

Do you see each day as a glorious opportunity to serve God and to do His will? Are you enthused about life, or do you struggle through each day giving scarcely a thought to God's blessings? Are you constantly praising God for His gifts, and are you sharing His Good News with the world? And are you excited about the possibilities for service that God has placed before you, whether at home, at work, at church, or at school? You should be.

You are the recipient of Christ's sacrificial love. Accept it enthusiastically and share it fervently. Jesus deserves your enthusiasm; the world deserves it; and you deserve the experience of sharing it.

God is the giver, and we are the receivers. And His richest gifts are bestowed not upon those who do the greatest things, but upon those who accept His abundance and His grace.

Hannah Whitall Smith

Living life with a consistent spiritual walk deeply influences those we love most.

Vonette Bright

Your light is the truth of the Gospel message itself as well as your witness as to Who Jesus is and what He has done for you. Don't hide it.

Anne Graham Lotz

We urgently need people who encourage and inspire us to move toward God and away from the world's enticing pleasures.

Jim Cymbala

GOD FIRST...OTHERS SECOND...

When you become genuinely enthused about your life and your faith, you'll guard your heart and improve your life.

DAY 38

RADICAL CHANGE REQUIRES DISCIPLINE

But I discipline my body and bring it into subjection, lest, when I have preached to others, I myself should become disqualified.

1 Corinthians 9:27 NKJV

Wise women understand the importance of discipline. In Proverbs 28:19, the message is clear: "Those who work their land will have plenty of food, but the ones who chase empty dreams instead will end up poor" (NCV).

If we work diligently and faithfully, we can expect a bountiful harvest. But we must never expect the harvest to precede the labor.

Poet Mary Frances Butts advised, "Build a little fence of trust around today. Fill each space with loving work, and therein stay." And her words still apply.

Thoughtful women understand that God doesn't reward laziness or misbehavior. To the contrary, God expects His children (of all ages) to lead disciplined lives . . . and when they do, He rewards them.

The alternative
to discipline is
disaster.

Vance Havner

WOMEN

Personal humility is a spiritual discipline and the hallmark of the service of Jesus.

Franklin Graham

True will power and courage are not on the battlefield, but in everyday conquests over our inertia, laziness, and boredom.

D. L. Moody

We set our eyes on the finish line, forgetting the past, and straining toward the mark of spiritual maturity and fruitfulness.

Vonette Bright

God has a present will for your life. It is neither chaotic nor utterly exhausting. In the midst of many good choices vying for your time, He will give you the discernment to recognize what is best.

Beth Moore

GOD FIRST...OTHERS SECOND...

If you choose to lead a disciplined lifestyle, your steps will be protected. If you choose to lead an undisciplined lifestyle, your steps will be misdirected.

DAY 39

STEWARDSHIP OF GOD'S GIFTS

Based on the gift they have received, everyone should use it to serve others, as good managers of the varied grace of God.

1 Peter 4:10 HCSB

The gifts that you possess are gifts from the Giver of all things good. Do you have a spiritual gift? Share it. Do you have a testimony about the things that Christ has done for you? Don't leave your story untold. Do you possess financial resources? Share them. Do you have particular talents? Hone your skills and use them for God's glory.

When you hoard the treasures that God has given you, you live in rebellion against His commandments. But, when you obey God by sharing His gifts freely and without fanfare, you invite Him to bless you more and more. Today, be a faithful steward of your talents and treasures. And then prepare yourself for even greater blessings that are sure to come.

WOMEN

The Lord has abundantly blessed me all of my life. I'm not trying to pay Him back for all of His wonderful gifts; I just realize that He gave them to me to give away.

Lisa Whelchel

When God crowns our merits, he is crowning nothing other than his gifts.

St. Augustine

If I find in myself a desire which no experience in this world can satisfy, the most probable explanation is that I was made for another world.

C. S. Lewis

If you want to discover your spiritual gifts, start obeying God. As you serve Him, you will find that He has given you the gifts that are necessary to follow through in obedience.

Anne Graham Lotz

What we are is God's gift to us. What we become is our gift to God.

Anonymous

GOD FIRST...OTHERS SECOND...

God has given you a unique array of talents and opportunities. The rest is up to you.

DAY 40

OPEN UP YOUR HEART

We know that all things work together for the good of those who love God: those who are called according to His purpose.

Romans 8:28 HCSB

C. S. Lewis observed, "A man's spiritual health is exactly proportional to his love for God." If we are to enjoy the spiritual health that God intends for us, we must praise Him, we must love Him, and we must obey Him.

When we worship God faithfully and obediently, we invite His love into our hearts. When we truly worship God, we allow Him to rule over our days and our lives. In turn, we grow to love God even more deeply as we sense His love for us.

St. Augustine wrote, "I love you, Lord, not doubtingly, but with absolute certainty. Your Word beat upon my heart until I fell in love with you, and now the universe and everything in it tells me to love you."

Today, open your heart to the Father. And let your obedience be a fitting response to His never-ending love.

WOMEN

Joy is a by-product not of happy circumstances, education or talent, but of a healthy relationship with God and a determination to love Him no matter what.

Barbara Johnson

Delighting thyself in the Lord is the sudden realization that He has become the desire of your heart.

Beth Moore

Loving Him means the thankful acceptance of all things that His love has appointed.

Elisabeth Elliot

When an honest soul can get still before the living Christ, we can still hear Him say simply and clearly, "Love the Lord your God with all your heart and with all your soul and with all your mind…and love one another as I have loved you."

Gloria Gaither

Telling the Lord how much you love Him and why is what praise and worship are all about.

Lisa Whelchel

GOD FIRST...OTHERS SECOND...

Because God first loved you, you should love Him. And one way that you demonstrate your love is by obeying Him.

DAY 41

STUDYING GOD'S BOOK

Like newborn infants, desire the unadulterated spiritual milk,
so that you may grow by it in your salvation.

1 Peter 2:2 HCSB

As a spiritual being, you have the potential to grow in your personal knowledge of the Lord every day that you live. You can do so through prayer, through worship, through an openness to God's Holy Spirit, and through a careful study of God's Holy Word.

Your Bible contains powerful prescriptions for everyday living. If you sincerely seek to walk with God, you should commit yourself to the thoughtful study of His teachings. The Bible can and should be your roadmap for every aspect of your life.

Do you seek to establish a closer relationship with your Heavenly Father? Then study His Word every day, with no exceptions. The Holy Bible is a priceless, one-of-a-kind gift from God. Treat it that way and read it that way.

Don't worry about what you do not understand of the Bible. Worry about what you do understand and do not live by.

Corrie ten Boom

The balance of affirmation and discipline, freedom and restraint, encouragement and warning is different for each child and season and generation, yet the absolutes of God's Word are necessary and trustworthy no matter how mercuric the time.

Gloria Gaither

The key to my understanding of the Bible is a personal relationship to Jesus Christ.

Oswald Chambers

The Bible is like no other book. Treat it that way!

Marie T. Freeman

If your Bible is falling apart, chances are your life is staying together.

Anonymous

GOD FIRST...OTHERS SECOND...

You're never too young—or too old—to become a serious student of God's Word.

DAY 42

LET GOD JUDGE

Do not judge, and you will not be judged. Do not condemn, and you will not be condemned. Forgive, and you will be forgiven.

Luke 6:37 HCSB

We have all fallen short of God's commandments, and He has forgiven us. We, too, must forgive others. And, we must refrain from judging them.

Are you one of those people who finds it easy to judge others? If so, it's time to change.

God does not need (or, for that matter, want) your help. Why? Because God is perfectly capable of judging the human heart . . . while you are not.

As Christians, we are warned that to judge others is to invite fearful consequences: to the extent we judge others, so, too, will we be judged by God. Let us refrain, then, from judging our neighbors. Instead, let us forgive them and love them in the same way that God has forgiven us.

Don't judge other
people more harshly
than you want God to
judge you.

Marie T. Freeman

Judging draws the judgment of others.

Catherine Marshall

An individual Christian may see fit to give up all sorts of things for special reasons—marriage, or meat, or beer, or cinema; but the moment he starts saying these things are bad in themselves, or looking down his nose at other people who do use them, he has taken the wrong turn.

C. S. Lewis

Christians think they are prosecuting attorneys or judges, when, in reality, God has called all of us to be witnesses.

Warren Wiersbe

On judgment day you'll meet Father God—not Mother Earth!

Anonymous

GOD FIRST...OTHERS SECOND...

If you're setting yourself up to be the judge and jury over other people, watch out! God will judge you in the same way you judge them. So don't be too hard on other people (unless, of course, you want God to be exactly that hard on you).

DAY 43

WHAT KIND OF EXAMPLE?

Be an example to the believers in word, in conduct, in love, in spirit, in faith, in purity.

1 Timothy 4:12 NKJV

Whether we like it or not, all of us are role models. Our friends and family members watch our actions and, as followers of Christ, we are obliged to act accordingly.

What kind of example are you? Are you the kind of woman whose life serves as a genuine example of righteousness? Are you a woman whose behavior serves as a positive role model for young people? Are you the kind of woman whose actions, day in and day out, are based upon kindness, faithfulness, and a love for the Lord? If so, you are not only blessed by God, but you are also a powerful force for good in a world that desperately needs positive influences such as yours.

Corrie ten Boom advised, "Don't worry about what you do not understand. Worry about what you do understand in the Bible but do not live by." And that's sound advice because our families and friends are watching . . . and so, for that matter, is God.

Your light is the truth of the Gospel message itself as well as your witness as to Who Jesus is and what He has done for you. Don't hide it.

Anne Graham Lotz

Living life with a consistent spiritual walk deeply influences those we love most.

Vonette Bright

In your desire to share the gospel, you may be the only Jesus someone else will ever meet. Be real and be involved with people.

Barbara Johnson

Our trustworthiness implies His trustworthiness.

Beth Moore

There is nothing anybody else can do that can stop God from using us...We can turn everything into a testimony.

Corrie ten Boom

GOD FIRST...OTHERS SECOND...

God wants you to be a positive role model. And that's what you should want, too.

DAY 44

BIG DREAMS

With God's power working in us, God can do much, much more than anything we can ask or imagine.

Ephesians 3:20 NCV

Are you willing to entertain the possibility that God has big plans in store for you? Hopefully so. Yet sometimes, especially if you've recently experienced a life-altering disappointment, you may find it difficult to envision a brighter future for yourself and your family. If so, it's time to reconsider your own capabilities . . . and God's.

Your Heavenly Father created you with unique gifts and untapped talents; your job is to tap them. When you do, you'll begin to feel an increasing sense of confidence in yourself and in your future.

It takes courage to dream big dreams. You will discover that courage when you do three things: accept the past, trust God to handle the future, and make the most of the time He has given you today.

Nothing is too difficult for God, and no dreams are too big for Him—not even yours. So start living—and dreaming—accordingly.

The future lies all before us. Shall it only be a slight advance upon what we usually do? Ought it not to be a bound, a leap forward to altitudes of endeavor and success undreamed of before?

Annie Armstrong

Allow your dreams a place in your prayers and plans. God-given dreams can help you move into the future He is preparing for you.

Barbara Johnson

Sometimes our dreams were so big that it took two people to dream them.

Marie T. Freeman

Always stay connected to people and seek out things that bring you joy. Dream with abandon. Pray confidently.

Barbara Johnson

If all things are possible with God, then all things are possible to him who believes in him.

Corrie ten Boom

GOD FIRST...OTHERS SECOND...

You can dream big dreams, but you can never out-dream God. His plans for you are even bigger than you can imagine.

DAY 45

GET INVOLVED IN A CHURCH

And I also say to you that you are Peter, and on this rock I will build My church, and the forces of Hades will not overpower it. I will give you the keys of the kingdom of heaven, and whatever you bind on earth will have been bound in heaven, and whatever you loose on earth will have been loosed in heaven.

Matthew 16:18–19 HCSB

If you want to build character, the church is a wonderful place to do it. Are you an active, contributing, member of your local fellowship? The answer to this simple question will have a profound impact on the direction of your spiritual journey and the content of your character.

If you are not currently engaged in a local church, you're missing out on an array of blessings that include, but are certainly not limited to, the life-lifting relationships that you can—and should—be experiencing with fellow believers.

So do yourself a favor: Find a congregation you're comfortable with, and join it. And once you've joined, don't just attend church out of habit. Go to church out of a sincere desire to know and worship God. When you do, you'll be blessed by the men and women who attend your fellowship, and you'll be blessed by your Creator. You deserve to attend church, and God deserves for you to attend church, so don't delay.

Someone has said that
the Church at its very worst
is better than the world at its best.

Gloria Gaither

WOMEN

Our churches are meant to be havens where the caste rules of the world do not apply.

Beth Moore

Be filled with the Holy Spirit; join a church where the members believe the Bible and know the Lord; seek the fellowship of other Christians; learn and be nourished by God's Word and His many promises. Conversion is not the end of your journey—it is only the beginning.

Corrie ten Boom

Every time a new person comes to God, every time someone's gifts find expression in the fellowship of believers, every time a family in need is surrounded by the caring church, the truth is affirmed anew: the Church triumphant is alive and well!

Gloria Gaither

GOD FIRST...OTHERS SECOND...

God intends for you to be actively involved in His church. Your intentions should be the same.

DAY 46

PAYING ATTENTION TO GOD

For where your treasure is, there your heart will be also.

Luke 12:34 HCSB

Who is in charge of your heart? Is it God, or is it something else? Have you given Christ your heart, your soul, your talents, your time, and your testimony? Or are you giving Him little more than a few hours each Sunday morning?

In the book of Exodus, God warns that we should place no gods before Him. Yet all too often, we place our Lord in second, third, or fourth place as we worship other things. When we unwittingly place possessions or relationships above our love for the Creator, we create big problems for ourselves.

Does God rule your heart? Make certain that the honest answer to this question is a resounding yes. In the life of every radical believer, God comes first. And that's precisely the place that He deserves in your heart.

God loves each of us
as if there were
only one of us.

St. Augustine

He treats us as sons, and all He asks in return is that we shall treat Him as a Father whom we can trust without anxiety. We must take the son's place of dependence and trust, and we must let Him keep the father's place of care and responsibility.

Hannah Whitall Smith

He is always thinking about us. We are before his eyes. The Lord's eye never sleeps, but is always watching out for our welfare. We are continually on his heart.

C. H. Spurgeon

In heaven, we will see that nothing, absolutely nothing, was wasted, and that every tear counted and every cry was heard.

Joni Eareckson Tada

GOD FIRST...OTHERS SECOND...

Because God is infinite and eternal, you cannot comprehend Him. But you can understand your need to praise Him, to love Him, and to obey His Word.

DAY 47

BE CAREFUL HOW YOU DIRECT YOUR THOUGHTS

Finally brothers, whatever is true, whatever is honorable, whatever is just, whatever is pure, whatever is lovely, whatever is commendable—if there is any moral excellence and if there is any praise—dwell on these things.

Philippians 4:8 HCSB

Thoughts are intensely powerful things. Our thoughts have the power to lift us up or drag us down; they have the power to energize us or deplete us, to inspire us to greater accomplishments, or to make those accomplishments impossible.

Bishop Fulton Sheen correctly observed, "The mind is like a clock that is constantly running down. It needs to be wound up daily with good thoughts." But sometimes, even for the most faithful believers, winding up our intellectual clocks is difficult indeed.

If negative thoughts have left you worried, exhausted, or both, it's time to readjust your thought patterns. Negative thinking is habit-forming; thankfully, so is positive thinking. And it's up to you to train your mind to focus on God's power and your possibilities. Both are far greater than you can imagine.

As we have by faith said no to sin, so we should by faith say yes to God and set our minds on things above, where Christ is seated in the heavenlies.

Vonette Bright

No more imperfect thoughts. No more sad memories. No more ignorance. My redeemed body will have a redeemed mind. Grant me a foretaste of that perfect mind as you mirror your thoughts in me today.

Joni Eareckson Tada

Attitude is the mind's paintbrush; it can color any situation.

Barbara Johnson

It is the thoughts and intents of the heart that shape a person's life.

John Eldredge

Preoccupy my thoughts with your praise beginning today.

Joni Eareckson Tada

GOD FIRST...OTHERS SECOND...

Either you can control your thoughts, or they most certainly will control you.

DAY 48

THE POWER OF PATIENCE

Trust in Him at all times, you people; pour out your heart before Him; God is a refuge for us.

Psalm 62:8 NKJV

Psalm 37:7 commands us to wait patiently for God. But as busy women in a fast-paced world, many of us find that waiting quietly for God is difficult. Why? Because we are fallible human beings seeking to live according to our own timetables, not God's. In our better moments, we realize that patience is not only a virtue, but it is also a commandment from God.

We human beings are impatient by nature. We know what we want, and we know exactly when we want it: NOW! But, God knows better. He has created a world that unfolds according to His plans, not our own. As believers, we must trust His wisdom and His goodness.

God instructs us to be patient in all things. We must be patient with our families, our friends, and our associates. We must also be patient with our Creator as He unfolds His plan for our lives. And that's as it should be. After all, think how patient God has been with us.

Let me encourage you to continue to wait with faith. God may not perform a miracle, but He is trustworthy to touch you and make you whole where there used to be a hole.

Lisa Whelchel

Waiting is the hardest kind of work, but God knows best, and we may joyfully leave all in His hands

Lottie Moon

Wisdom always waits for the right time to act, while emotion always pushes for action right now.

Joyce Meyer

How do you wait upon the Lord? First you must learn to sit at His feet and take time to listen to His words.

Kay Arthur

When we read of the great Biblical leaders, we see that it was not uncommon for God to ask them to wait, not just a day or two, but for years, until God was ready for them to act.

Gloria Gaither

GOD FIRST...OTHERS SECOND...

When you learn to be more patient with others, you'll make your world—and your heart—a better place.

DAY 49

ASK HIM FOR THE THINGS YOU NEED

You do not have because you do not ask.

James 4:2 HCSB

God gives the gifts; we, as believers, should accept them—but oftentimes, we don't. Why? Because we fail to trust our Heavenly Father completely, and because we are, at times, surprisingly stubborn. Luke 11 teaches us that God does not withhold spiritual gifts from those who ask. Our obligation, quite simply, is to ask for them.

Are you a woman who asks God to move mountains in your life, or are you expecting Him to stumble over molehills? Whatever the size of your challenges, God is big enough to handle them. Ask for His help today, with faith and with fervor, and then watch in amazement as your mountains begin to move.

God will help us become the people
we are meant to be,
if only we will ask Him.

Hannah Whitall Smith

When will we realize that we're not troubling God with our questions and concerns? His heart is open to hear us—his touch nearer than our next thought—as if no one in the world existed but us. Our very personal God wants to hear from us personally.

Gigi Graham Tchividjian

When trials come your way—as inevitably they will—do not run away. Run to your God and Father.

Kay Arthur

Often I have made a request of God with earnest pleadings even backed up with Scripture, only to have Him say "No" because He had something better in store.

Ruth Bell Graham

By asking in Jesus' name, we're making a request not only in His authority, but also for His interests and His benefit.

Shirley Dobson

GOD FIRST...OTHERS SECOND...

If you sincerely want to guard your steps, ask for God's help.

DAY 50

YOU AND YOUR FAMILY

But if any widow has children or grandchildren, they should learn to practice their religion toward their own family first and to repay their parents, for this pleases God.

1 Timothy 5:4 HCSB

As every woman knows, family life is a mixture of conversations, mediations, irritations, deliberations, commiserations, frustrations, negotiations and celebrations. In other words, the life of the typical mom is incredibly varied.

Certainly, in the life of every family, there are moments of frustration and disappointment. Lots of them. But, for those who are lucky enough to live in the presence of a close-knit, caring clan, the rewards far outweigh the frustrations. That's why we pray fervently for our family members, and that's why we love them despite their faults.

No family is perfect, and neither is yours. But, despite the inevitable challenges and occasional hurt feelings of family life, your clan is God's gift to you. That little band of men, women, kids, and babies is a priceless treasure on temporary loan from the Father above. Give thanks to the Giver for the gift of family…and act accordingly.

A home is a place where we find direction.

Gigi Graham Tchividjian

One way or the other, God, who thought up the family in the first place, has the very best idea of how to bring sense to the chaos of broken relationships we see all around us. I really believe that if I remain still and listen a lot, He will share some solutions with me so I can share them with others.

Jill Briscoe

Living life with a consistent spiritual walk deeply influences those we love most.

Vonette Bright

Live in the present and make the most of your opportunities to enjoy your family and friends.

Barbara Johnson

The family that prays together, stays together.

Anonymous

GOD FIRST...OTHERS SECOND...

Your family is a precious gift from above, a gift that should be treasured, nurtured, and loved.

DAY 51

BE STILL

Be still, and know that I am God.

Psalm 46:10 NKJV

In the first chapter of Mark, we read that in the darkness of the early morning hours, Jesus went to a solitary place and prayed. So, too, should we. But sometimes, finding quiet moments of solitude is difficult indeed.

We live in a noisy world, a world filled with distractions, frustrations, and complications. But if we allow the distractions of a clamorous world to separate us from God's peace, we do ourselves a profound disservice.

If we seek to maintain righteous minds and compassionate hearts, we must take time each day for prayer and for meditation. We must make ourselves still in the presence of our Creator. We must quiet our minds and our hearts so that we can sense God's will, God's love, and God's Son.

Are you one of those busy women who rush through the day with scarcely a single moment for quiet contemplation and prayer? If so, it's time to reorder your priorities.

Has the busy pace of life robbed you of the peace that might otherwise be yours through Jesus Christ? Nothing is more important than the time you spend with your Savior. So be still and claim the inner peace that is your spiritual birthright: the peace of Jesus Christ. It is offered freely; it has been paid for in full; it is yours for the asking. So ask. And then share.

The manifold rewards of a serious,
consistent prayer life demonstrate clearly
that time with our Lord
should be our first priority.

Shirley Dobson

WOMEN

The Lord Jesus, available to people much of the time, left them, sometimes a great while before day, to go up to the hills where He could commune in solitude with His Father.

Elisabeth Elliot

I need the spiritual revival that comes from spending quiet time alone with Jesus in prayer and in thoughtful meditation on His Word.

Anne Graham Lotz

If you, too, will learn to wait upon God, to get alone with Him, and remain silent so that you can hear His voice when He is ready to speak to you, what a difference it will make in your life!

Kay Arthur

In the center of a hurricane there is absolute quiet and peace. There is no safer place than in the center of the will of God.

Corrie ten Boom

GOD FIRST...OTHERS SECOND...

Be still and listen to God. He has something important to say to you.

DAY 52

YOUR VERY BRIGHT FUTURE

"For I know the plans I have for you"—[this is] the Lord's declaration—"plans for [your] welfare, not for disaster, to give you a future and a hope."

Jeremiah 29:11 HCSB

How bright is your future? Well, if you are a faithful believer, God's plans for you are so bright that you'd better wear shades. But here's an important question: How bright do you believe your future to be? Are you expecting a terrific tomorrow, or are you dreading a terrible one? The answer you give will have a powerful impact on the way tomorrow turns out.

Do you trust in the ultimate goodness of God's plan for your life? Will you face tomorrow's challenges with optimism and hope? You should. After all, God created you for a very important reason: His reason. And you still have important work to do: His work.

Today, as you live in the present and look to the future, remember that God has an amazing plan for you. Act—and believe—accordingly.

We spend our lives
dreaming of
the future,
not realizing that
a little of it slips
away every day.

Barbara Johnson

You can look forward with hope, because one day there will be no more separation, no more scars, and no more suffering in My Father's House. It's the home of your dreams!

Anne Graham Lotz

Do not limit the limitless God! With Him, face the future unafraid because you are never alone.

Mrs. Charles E. Cowman

Every experience God gives us, every person he brings into our lives, is the perfect preparation for the future that only he can see.

Corrie ten Boom

Our future may look fearfully intimidating, yet we can look up to the Engineer of the Universe, confident that nothing escapes His attention or slips out of the control of those strong hands.

Elisabeth Elliot

GOD FIRST...OTHERS SECOND...

Even when the world seems dark, the future is bright for those who look to the Son.

DAY 53

EXPERIENCING GOD'S ABUNDANCE

I have come that they may have life, and that they may have it more abundantly.

John 10:10 NKJV

The familiar words of John 10:10 should serve as a daily reminder: Christ came to this earth so that we might experience His abundance, His love, and His gift of eternal life. But Christ does not force Himself upon us; we must claim His gifts for ourselves.

Every woman knows that some days are so busy and so hurried that abundance seems a distant promise. It is not. Every day, we can claim the spiritual abundance that God promises for our lives…and we should.

Hannah Whitall Smith spoke for believers of every generation when she observed, "God is the giver, and we are the receivers. And His richest gifts are bestowed not upon those who do the greatest things, but upon those who accept His abundance and His grace."

Christ is, indeed, the Giver. Will you accept His gifts today?

God's riches are beyond anything we could ask or even dare to imagine! If my life gets gooey and stale, I have no excuse.

Barbara Johnson

Yes, we were created for His holy pleasure, but we will ultimately—if not immediately—find much pleasure in His pleasure.

Beth Moore

It would be wrong to have a "poverty complex," for to think ourselves paupers is to deny either the King's riches or to deny our being His children.

Catherine Marshall

Jesus intended for us to be overwhelmed by the blessings of regular days. He said it was the reason he had come: "I am come that they might have life, and that they might have it more abundantly."

Gloria Gaither

GOD FIRST...OTHERS SECOND...

God wants to shower you with abundance—your job is to let Him.

DAY 54

TRUST GOD'S WISDOM

Insight is a fountain of life for its possessor, but folly is the instruction of fools.

Proverbs 16:22 HCSB

Where will you place your trust today? Will you trust in the wisdom of fallible men and women, or will you place your faith in God's perfect wisdom? When you decide whom to trust, you will then know how best to respond to the challenges of the coming day.

Are you tired? Discouraged? Fearful? Be comforted and trust God. Are you worried or anxious? Be confident in God's power and trust His Holy Word. Are you confused? Listen to the quiet voice of your Heavenly Father. He is not a God of confusion. Talk with Him; listen to Him; trust Him. He is steadfast, and He is your Protector . . . forever.

We get into trouble when we think
we know what to do and we stop
asking God if we're doing it.

Stormie Omartian

Yielding to the will of God is simply letting His Holy Spirit have His way in our lives.

Shirley Dobson

If you are struggling to make some difficult decisions right now that aren't specifically addressed in the Bible, don't make a choice based on what's right for someone else. You are the Lord's and He will make sure you do what's right.

Lisa Whelchel

Make God's will the focus of your life day by day. If you seek to please Him and Him alone, you'll find yourself satisfied with life.

Kay Arthur

The will of God is never exactly what you expect it to be. It may seem to be much worse, but in the end it's going to be a lot better and a lot bigger.

Elisabeth Elliot

GOD FIRST...OTHERS SECOND...

God's wisdom is perfect, and it's available to you. So if you want to become wise, become a student of God's Word and a follower of His Son.

DAY 55

THE DANGERS OF MODERN MEDIA

Do not love the world or the things that belong to the world. If anyone loves the world, love for the Father is not in him.

1 John 2:15 HCSB

Sometimes it's hard being a woman of faith especially when the world keeps pumping out messages that are contrary to your beliefs.

Beware! The media is working around the clock in an attempt to rearrange your priorities. The media says that appearance is all-important, that thinness is all-important, and that social standing is all-important. But guess what? Those messages are untrue. The important things in life have little to do with appearances. The all-important things in life have to do with your faith, your family, and your future. Period.

Because you live in the 21st century, you are relentlessly bombarded by media messages that are contrary to your faith. Take those messages with a grain of salt—or better yet, don't take them at all.

Every Christian is a contradiction to this old world. He crosses it at every point. He goes against the grain from beginning to end. From the day that he is born again until the day that he goes on to be with the Lord, he must stand against the current of a world always going the other way.

Vance Havner

A fish would never be happy living on land, because it was made for water. An eagle could never feel satisfied if it wasn't allowed to fly. You will never feel completely satisfied on earth, because you were made for more.

Rick Warren

Our fight is not against any physical enemy; it is against organizations and powers that are spiritual. We must struggle against sin all our lives, but we are assured we will win.

Corrie ten Boom

It is impossible to please God doing things motivated by and produced by the flesh.

Bill Bright

GOD FIRST...OTHERS SECOND...

The popular media has a way of attacking your senses and your heart. Approach the media with care.

DAY 56

CELEBRATING LIFE

This is the day the Lord has made; let us rejoice and be glad in it.

Psalm 118:24 HCSB

The 100th Psalm reminds us that the entire earth should "Shout for joy to the Lord." As God's children, we are blessed beyond measure, but sometimes, as busy women living in a demanding world, we are slow to count our gifts and even slower to give thanks to the Giver.

Our blessings include life and health, family and friends, freedom and possessions—for starters. And, the gifts we receive from God are multiplied when we share them. May we always give thanks to God for His blessings, and may we always demonstrate our gratitude by sharing our gifts with others.

The 118th Psalm reminds us that, "This is the day which the LORD has made; let us rejoice and be glad in it" (v. 24, NASB). May we celebrate this day and the One who created it.

According to Jesus,
it is God's will that
His children be filled
with the joy of life.

Catherine Marshall

WOMEN

If you can forgive the person you were, accept the person you are, and believe in the person you will become, you are headed for joy. So celebrate your life.

Barbara Johnson

Christ is the secret, the source, the substance, the center, and the circumference of all true and lasting gladness.

Mrs. Charles E. Cowman

When the dream of our heart is one that God has planted there, a strange happiness flows into us. At that moment, all of the spiritual resources of the universe are released to help us. Our praying is then at one with the will of God and becomes a channel for the Creator's purposes for us and our world.

Catherine Marshall

Joy is a by-product not of happy circumstances, education or talent, but of a healthy relationship with God and a determination to love Him no matter what.

Barbara Johnson

GOD FIRST...OTHERS SECOND...

Every day should be a cause for celebration. By celebrating the gift of life, you protect your heart from the dangers of pessimism, regret, hopelessness, and bitterness.

DAY 57

IF YOU REACH OUT TO GOD • • •

Draw near to God, and He will draw near to you.

James 4:8 HCSB

Do you ever wonder if God is really "right here, right now"? Do you wonder if God hears your prayers, if He understands your feelings, or if He really knows your heart? If so, you're not alone: lots of very faithful Christians have experienced periods of doubt. In fact, some of the biggest heroes in the Bible had plenty of doubts—and so, perhaps, will you. But when you have doubts, remember this: God isn't on a coffee break, and He hasn't moved out of town. God isn't taking a long vacation, and He isn't snoozing on the couch. He's right here, right now, listening to your thoughts and prayers, watching over your every move.

If you'd like to get to know God a little bit better, He's always available—always ready to listen to your prayers, and always ready to speak to your heart. Are you ready to talk to Him? If so, congratulations. If not, what are you waiting for?

WOMEN

Here is our opportunity: we cannot see God, but we can see Christ. Christ was not only the Son of God, but He was the Father. Whatever Christ was, that God is.

Hannah Whitall Smith

You cannot grow spiritually until you have the assurance that Christ is in your life.

Vonette Bright

The only way we can be convinced of Who Jesus is, is through the enlightenment we have received from the Holy Spirit.

Anne Graham Lotz

Christians have spent their whole lives mastering all sorts of principles, done their duty, carried on the programs of their church...and never known God intimately, heart to heart.

John Eldredge

GOD FIRST...OTHERS SECOND...

If you'd like to get to know God a little better, talk to Him more often. The more often you speak to Him, the more often He'll speak to you.

DAY 58

HOLINESS BEFORE HAPPINESS

Blessed are those who hunger and thirst for righteousness, because they will be filled.

Matthew 5:6 HCSB

How do we live a life that is "right with God"? By accepting God's Son and obeying His commandments. Accepting Christ is a decision that we make one time; following in His footsteps requires thousands of decisions each day.

Whose steps will you follow today? Will you honor God as you strive to follow His Son? Or will you join the lockstep legion that seeks to discover happiness and fulfillment through worldly means? If you are righteous and wise, you will follow Christ. You will follow Him today and every day. You will seek to walk in His footsteps without reservation or doubt. When you do so, you will be "right with God" precisely because you are walking aright with His only begotten Son.

WOMEN

Holiness isn't in a style of dress. It's not a matter of rules and regulations. It's a way of life that emanates quietness and rest, joy in family, shared pleasures with friends, the help of a neighbor—and the hope of a Savior.

Joni Eareckson Tada

Holiness has never been the driving force of the majority. It is, however, mandatory for anyone who wants to enter the kingdom.

Elisabeth Elliot

How little people know who think that holiness is dull. When one meets the real thing, it's irresistible.

C. S. Lewis

Our afflictions are designed not to break us but to bend us toward the eternal and the holy.

Barbara Johnson

GOD FIRST...OTHERS SECOND...

God is holy and wants you to be holy. You should make certain that your response to God's love is obedience to Him.

DAY 59

HAVE THE COURAGE TO TRUST GOD

Trust in the Lord with all your heart, and do not rely on your own understanding; think about Him in all your ways, and He will guide you on the right paths.

Proverbs 3:5-6 HCSB

When our dreams come true and our plans prove successful, we find it easy to thank our Creator and easy to trust His divine providence. But in times of sorrow or hardship, we may find ourselves questioning God's plans for our lives.

On occasion, you will confront circumstances that trouble you to the very core of your soul. It is during these difficult days that you must find the wisdom and the courage to trust your Heavenly Father despite your circumstances.

Are you a woman who seeks God's blessings for yourself and your family? Then trust Him. Trust Him with your relationships. Trust Him with your priorities. Follow His commandments and pray for His guidance. Trust your Heavenly Father day by day, moment by moment—in good times and in trying times. Then, wait patiently for

God's revelations . . . and prepare yourself for the abundance and peace that will most certainly be yours when you do.

Brother, is your faith looking upward today?
Trust in the promise of the Savior.
Sister, is the light shining bright on your way?
Trust in the promise of thy Lord.

Fanny Crosby

Do not be afraid, then, that if you trust, or tell others to trust, the matter will end there. Trust is only the beginning and the continual foundation. When we trust Him, the Lord works, and His work is the important part of the whole matter.

Hannah Whitall Smith

Sometimes the very essence of faith is trusting God in the midst of things He knows good and well we cannot comprehend.

Beth Moore

Are you serious about wanting God's guidance to become the person he wants you to be? The first step is to tell God that you know you can't manage your own life; that you need his help.

Catherine Marshall

Never be afraid to trust an unknown future to a known God.

Corrie ten Boom

GOD FIRST...OTHERS SECOND...

Because God is trustworthy and because He has made promises to you that He intends to keep—you are protected.

DAY 60

LET GOD GUIDE THE WAY

The true children of God are those who let God's Spirit lead them.

Romans 8:14 NCV

The Bible promises that God will guide you if you let Him. Your job, of course, is to let Him. But sometimes, you will be tempted to do otherwise. Sometimes, you'll be tempted to go along with the crowd; other times, you'll be tempted to do things your way, not God's way. When you feel those temptations, resist them.

What will you allow to guide you through the coming day: your own desires (or, for that matter, the desires of your friends)? Or will you allow God to lead the way? The answer should be obvious. You should let God be your guide. When you entrust your life to Him completely and without reservation, God will give you the strength to meet any challenge, the courage to face any trial, and the wisdom to live in His righteousness. So trust Him today and seek His guidance. When you do, your next step will be the right one.

Are you serious about wanting God's guidance to become a personal reality in your life? The first step is to tell God that you know you can't manage your own life; that you need his help.

Catherine Marshall

God's guidance is even more important than common sense. I can declare that the deepest darkness is outshone by the light of Jesus.

Corrie ten Boom

We have ample evidence that the Lord is able to guide. The promises cover every imaginable situation. All we need to do is to take the hand he stretches out.

Elisabeth Elliot

Experience has taught me that the Shepherd is far more willing to show His sheep the path than the sheep are to follow. He is endlessly merciful, patient, tender, and loving. If we, His stupid and wayward sheep, really want to be led, we will without fail be led. Of that I am sure.

Elisabeth Elliot

GOD FIRST...OTHERS SECOND...

If you're wise, you'll allow God to guide you today and every day of your life. When you pray for guidance, God will give it.

DAY 61

HIS DISCIPLE

He has told you men what is good and what it is the Lord requires of you: Only to act justly, to love faithfulness, and to walk humbly with your God.

Micah 6:8 HCSB

When Jesus addressed His disciples, He warned that each one must "take up his cross and follow Me." The disciples must have known exactly what the Master meant. In Jesus' day, prisoners were forced to carry their own crosses to the location where they would be put to death. Thus, Christ's message was clear: in order to follow Him, Christ's disciples must deny themselves and, instead, trust Him completely. Nothing has changed since then.

If we are to be disciples of Christ, we must trust Him and place Him at the very center of our beings. Jesus never comes "next." He is always first. The paradox, of course, is that only by sacrificing ourselves to Him do we gain salvation for ourselves.

Do you seek to be a worthy disciple of Christ? Then pick up His cross today and every day that you live. When you do, He will bless you now and forever.

Jesus challenges you
and me to keep our
focus daily on the
cross of His will
if we want to be His
disciples.

Anne Graham Lotz

WOMEN

Be filled with the Holy Spirit; join a church where the members believe the Bible and know the Lord; seek the fellowship of other Christians; learn and be nourished by God's Word and His many promises. Conversion is not the end of your journey—it is only the beginning.

Corrie ten Boom

When Jesus put the little child in the midst of His disciples, He did not tell the little child to become like His disciples; He told the disciples to become like the little child.

Ruth Bell Graham

You cannot cooperate with Jesus in becoming what He wants you to become and simultaneously be what the world desires to make you. If you would say, "Take the world but give me Jesus," then you must deny yourself and take up your cross. The simple truth is that your "self" must be put to death in order for you to get to the point where for you to live is Christ. What will it be? The world and you, or Jesus and you? You do have a choice to make.

Kay Arthur

GOD FIRST...OTHERS SECOND...

Jesus invites you to become His disciple . . . and the rest is up to you.

DAY 62

CHOOSING TO BEHAVE DIFFERENTLY

As God's slaves, live as free people, but don't use your freedom as a way to conceal evil.

1 Peter 2:16 HCSB

Life is a series of choices. Each day, we make countless decisions that can bring us closer to God...or not. When we live according to God's commandments, we earn for ourselves the abundance and peace that He intends for our lives. But, when we turn our backs upon God by ignoring Him—or by disobeying Him—we bring needless pain and suffering upon ourselves and our families.

Do you want God's peace and His blessings? Then obey Him. When you're faced with a difficult choice or a powerful temptation, seek God's counsel and trust the counsel He gives. Invite God into your heart and live according to His commandments. And when God speaks to you through that little quiet voice that He has placed in your heart, listen. When you do, you will be blessed today, and tomorrow, and forever. And you'll discover that happiness means living in accordance with your beliefs. No exceptions.

WOMEN

When your good behavior speaks for itself . . . don't interrupt.

Anonymous

Although God causes all things to work together for good for His children, He still holds us accountable for our behavior.

Kay Arthur

There may be no trumpet sound or loud applause when we make a right decision, just a calm sense of resolution and peace.

Gloria Gaither

Study the Bible and observe how the persons behaved and how God dealt with them. There is explicit teaching on every condition of life.

Corrie ten Boom

GOD FIRST...OTHERS SECOND...

How can you guard your steps? By walking with Jesus every day of your life.

DAY 63

CRITICS BEWARE

Don't criticize one another, brothers. He who criticizes a brother or judges his brother criticizes the law and judges the law. But if you judge the law, you are not a doer of the law but a judge.

James 4:11 HCSB

From experience, we know that it is easier to criticize than to correct; we understand that it is easier to find faults than solutions; and we realize that excessive criticism is usually destructive, not productive. Yet the urge to criticize others remains a powerful temptation for most of us.

In the book of James, we are issued a clear warning: "Don't criticize one another, brothers" (4:11). Undoubtedly, James understood the paralyzing power of chronic negativity, and so should we.

Negativity is highly contagious: we give it to others who, in turn, give it back to us. This cycle can be broken by positive thoughts, heartfelt prayers, and encouraging words. As thoughtful servants of a loving God, we can use the transforming power of Christ's love to break the chains of negativity. And we should.

WOMEN

When something robs you of your peace of mind, ask yourself if it is worth the energy you are expending on it. If not, then put it out of your mind in an act of discipline. Every time the thought of "it" returns, refuse it.

Kay Arthur

Discouraged people, if they must be discouraged, ought, at least, to keep their discouragements to themselves, hidden away in the privacy of their own bosoms lest they should discourage the hearts of their brethren.

Hannah Whitall Smith

Being critical of others, including God, is one way we try to avoid facing and judging our own sins.

Warren Wiersbe

The scrutiny we give other people should be for ourselves.

Oswald Chambers

After one hour in heaven, we shall be ashamed that we ever grumbled.

Vance Havner

GOD FIRST...OTHERS SECOND...

If you're too critical of other people—or of yourself—it's time to become more forgiving and less judgmental.

WHAT IS YOUR FOCUS?

Let your eyes look forward; fix your gaze straight ahead.

Proverbs 4:25 HCSB

This day—and every day hereafter—is a chance to celebrate the life that God has given you. It's also a chance to give thanks to the One who has offered you more blessings than you can possibly count. What is your focus today? Are you willing to focus your thoughts and energies on God's blessings and upon His will for your life? Or will you turn your thoughts to other things?

Today, why not focus your thoughts on the joy that is rightfully yours in Christ? Why not take time to celebrate God's glorious creation? Why not trust your hopes instead of your fears? When you do, you will think optimistically about yourself and your world . . . and you can then share your optimism with others. They'll be better for it, and so will you. But not necessarily in that order.

Measure the size of the obstacles against the size of God.

Beth Moore

We need to stop focusing on our lacks and stop giving out excuses and start looking at and listening to Jesus.

Anne Graham Lotz

What is your focus today? Joy comes when it is Jesus first, others second...then you.

Kay Arthur

Don't let worry rob you of the joy that is rightfully yours. God is in heaven, and He knows your every need. Focus on God and His provisions, and watch gratefully as the worries of today begin to fade away.

Marie T. Freeman

Paul did one thing. Most of us dabble in forty things. Are you a doer or a dabbler?

Vance Havner

GOD FIRST...OTHERS SECOND...

When you focus on God's promises, the world's troubles grow increasingly dim.

DAY 65

FOLLOW HIM

If anyone serves Me, let him follow Me; and where I am, there My servant will be also. If anyone serves Me, him My Father will honor.

John 12:26 NKJV

Jesus walks with you. Are you walking with Him? Hopefully, you will choose to walk with Him today and every day of your life.

Jesus loved you so much that He endured unspeakable humiliation and suffering for you. How will you respond to Christ's sacrifice? Will you take up His cross and follow Him (Luke 9:23), or will you choose another path? When you place your hopes squarely at the foot of the cross, when you place Jesus squarely at the center of your life, you will be blessed. If you seek to be a worthy disciple of Jesus, you must acknowledge that He never comes "next." He is always first.

Do you hope to fulfill God's purpose for your life? Do you seek a life of abundance and peace? Do you intend to be a Christian, not just in name, but in deed? Then follow Christ. Follow Him by picking up His cross daily. When you do, you will quickly discover that Christ's love has the power to change everything, including you.

WOMEN

Peter said, "No, Lord!" But he had to learn that one cannot say "No" while saying "Lord" and that one cannot say "Lord" while saying "No."

Corrie ten Boom

The love life of the Christian is a crucial battleground. There, if nowhere else, it will be determined who is Lord: the world, the self, and the devil—or the Lord Christ.

Elisabeth Elliot

Will you, with a glad and eager surrender, hand yourself and all that concerns you over into his hands? If you will do this, your soul will begin to know something of the joy of union with Christ.

Hannah Whitall Smith

The Christian faith is meant to be lived moment by moment. It isn't some broad, general outline—it's a long walk with a real Person. Details count: passing thoughts, small sacrifices, a few encouraging words, little acts of kindness, brief victories over nagging sins.

Joni Eareckson Tada

GOD FIRST...OTHERS SECOND...

It takes a radical commitment and significant sacrifices to really follow Jesus. And it's worth it.

DAY 66

CHOOSING TO BE KIND

And may the Lord make you increase and abound in love to one another and to all.

1 Thessalonians 3:12 NKJV

Christ showed His love for us by willingly sacrificing His own life so that we might have eternal life: "But God demonstrates his own love for us in this: While we were still sinners, Christ died for us" (Romans 5:8 NIV). We, as Christ's followers, are challenged to share His love with kind words on our lips and praise in our hearts.

Just as Christ has been—and will always be—the ultimate friend to His flock, so should we be Christlike in the kindness and generosity that we show toward others, especially those who are most in need.

When we walk each day with Jesus—and obey the commandments found in God's Holy Word —we become worthy ambassadors for Christ. When we share the love of Christ, we share a priceless gift with the world. As His servants, we must do no less.

WOMEN

Kindness in this world will do much to help others, not only to come into the light, but also to grow in grace day by day.

Fanny Crosby

All kindness and good deeds, we must keep silent. The result will be an inner reservoir of personality power.

Catherine Marshall

The attitude of kindness is everyday stuff like a great pair of sneakers. Not frilly. Not fancy. Just plain and comfortable.

Barbara Johnson

When we Christians are too busy to care for each other, we're simply too busy for our own good . . . and for God's.

Marie T. Freeman

GOD FIRST...OTHERS SECOND...

Kind words have echoes that last a lifetime and beyond.

DAY 67

TOO BUSY?

Be careful not to forget the Lord.

Deuteronomy 6:12 HCSB

Has the busy pace of life robbed you of the peace that might otherwise be yours through Jesus Christ? If so, you are simply too busy for your own good. Through His Son Jesus, God offers you a peace that passes human understanding, but He won't force His peace upon you; in order to experience it, you must slow down long enough to sense His presence and His love.

Today, as a gift to yourself, to your family, and to the world, slow down and claim the inner peace that is your spiritual birthright: the peace of Jesus Christ. It is offered freely; it has been paid for in full; it is yours for the asking. So ask. And then share.

WOMEN

In our tense, uptight society where folks are rushing to make appointments they have already missed, a good laugh can be as refreshing as a cup of cold water in the desert.

Barbara Johnson

Frustration is not the will of God. There is time to do anything and everything that God wants us to do.

Elisabeth Elliot

If you can't seem to find time for God, then you're simply too busy for your own good. God is never too busy for you, and you should never be too busy for Him.

Marie T. Freeman

The demand of every day kept me so busy that I subconsciously equated my busyness with commitment to Christ.

Vonette Bright

GOD FIRST...OTHERS SECOND...

The world wants to grab every spare minute of your time, but God wants some of your time, too. When in doubt, trust God.

DAY 68

BE AWARE OF
YOUR BLESSINGS

*Therefore, get your minds ready for action, being self-
disciplined, and set your hope completely on the grace to be
brought to you at the revelation of Jesus Christ.*

1 Peter 1:13 HCSB

Psalm 145 makes this promise: "The LORD is gracious and
compassionate, slow to anger and rich in love. The LORD
is good to all; he has compassion on all he has made"
(vv. 8-9 NIV). As God's children, we are blessed beyond
measure, but sometimes, as busy women in a demanding
world, we are slow to count our gifts and even slower to
give thanks to the Giver. Our blessings include life and
health, family and friends, freedom and possessions—for
starters. And, the gifts we receive from God are multiplied
when we share them with others. May we always give
thanks to God for our blessings, and may we always demonstrate our gratitude by sharing them.

WOMEN

Jesus intended for us to be overwhelmed by the blessings of regular days. He said it was the reason he had come: "I am come that they might have life, and that they might have it more abundantly."

Gloria Gaither

Do we not continually pass by blessings innumerable without notice, and instead fix our eyes on what we feel to be our trials and our losses, and think and talk about these until our whole horizon is filled with them, and we almost begin to think we have no blessings at all?

Hannah Whitall Smith

Think of the blessings we so easily take for granted: Life itself; preservation from danger; every bit of health we enjoy; every hour of liberty; the ability to see, to hear, to speak, to think, and to imagine all this comes from the hand of God.

Billy Graham

GOD FIRST...OTHERS SECOND...

God gives us countless blessings. We, in turn, should give Him our thanks and our praise.

DAY 69

PROBLEM-SOLVING 101

People who do what is right may have many problems, but the Lord will solve them all.

Psalm 34:19 NCV

Face facts: the upcoming day will not be problem-free. In fact, your life can be viewed as an exercise in problem-solving. The question is not whether you will encounter problems; the real question is how you will choose to address them.

When it comes to solving the problems of everyday living, we often know precisely what needs to be done, but we may be slow in doing it—especially if what needs to be done is difficult or uncomfortable. So we put off till tomorrow what should be done today.

The words of Psalm 34 remind us that the Lord solves problems for "people who do what is right." And usually, doing "what is right" means doing the uncomfortable work of confronting our problems sooner rather than later. So with no further ado, let the problem-solving begin . . . now.

When you are in deep water—trust the One who walked on it.

Anonymous

No matter how heavy the burden, daily strength is given, so I expect we need not give ourselves any concern as to what the outcome will be. We must simply go forward.

Annie Armstrong

"But he knows the way that I take; when he has tested me, I will come forth as gold" (Job 23:10 NIV). We will all "come forth as gold" if we understand that God is sovereign and knows what is best, even when we cannot understand what is happening at the time.

Shirley Dobson

God helps those who help themselves, but there are times when we are quite incapable of helping ourselves. That's when God stoops down and gathers us in His arms like a mother lifts a sick child, and does for us what we cannot do for ourselves.

Ruth Bell Graham

GOD FIRST...OTHERS SECOND...

Today, think about the wisdom of tackling your problems sooner rather than later. Remember that "this, too, will pass," but whatever "it" is will pass more quickly if you spend more time solving your problems and less time fretting about them.

DAY 70

BE A CHEERFUL CHRISTIAN

A cheerful heart has a continual feast.

Proverbs 15:15 HCSB

On some days, as every woman knows, it's hard to be cheerful. Sometimes, as the demands of the world increase and our energy sags, we feel less like "cheering up" and more like "tearing up." But even in our darkest hours, we can turn to God, and He will give us comfort.

Few things in life are more sad, or, for that matter, more absurd, than a grumpy Christian. Christ promises us lives of abundance and joy, but He does not force His joy upon us. We must claim His joy for ourselves, and when we do, Jesus, in turn, fills our spirits with His power and His love.

How can we receive from Christ the joy that is rightfully ours? By giving Him what is rightfully His: our hearts and our souls.

When we earnestly commit ourselves to the Savior of mankind, and when we place Jesus at the center of our lives and trust Him as our personal Savior, He will transform us, not just for today, but for all eternity. Then we, as God's children, can share Christ's joy and His message with a world that needs both.

We may run, walk, stumble, drive, or fly, but let us never lose sight of the reason for the journey, or miss a chance to see a rainbow on the way.

Gloria Gaither

When we bring sunshine into the lives of others, we're warmed by it ourselves. When we spill a little happiness, it splashes on us.

Barbara Johnson

Cheerfulness is its own reward—but not its only reward.

Criswell Freeman

God is good, and heaven is forever. And if those two facts don't cheer you up, nothing will.

Marie T. Freeman

Be assured, my dear friend, that it is no joy to God in seeing you with a dreary countenance.

C. H. Spurgeon

GOD FIRST...OTHERS SECOND...

Cheerfulness is its own reward—but not its only reward.

DAY 71

THE WISDOM TO BE GENEROUS

Freely you have received, freely give.

Matthew 10:8 NKJV

God's heart overflows with generosity and mercy. And as believers in a loving God, we must, to the best of our abilities, imitate our Heavenly Father. Because God has been so incredibly generous with us, we, in turn must be generous with others.

Jesus has much to teach us about generosity. He teaches that the most esteemed men and women are not the self-congratulatory leaders of society but are, instead, the humblest of servants (Matthew 23:11-12).

If you were being graded on generosity, how would you score? Would you earn "A"s in philanthropy and humility? Hopefully so. But if your grades could stand a little improvement, today is the perfect day to begin.

Today, you may feel the urge to hoard your blessings. Don't do it. Instead, give generously to your neighbors, and do so without fanfare. Find a need and fill it...humbly. Lend a helping hand and share a word of kindness... anonymously. This is God's way.

When somebody needs a helping hand, he doesn't need it tomorrow or the next day. He needs it now, and that's exactly when you should offer to help. Good deeds, if they are really good, happen sooner rather than later.

Marie T. Freeman

Just pray for a tough hide and a tender heart.

Ruth Bell Graham

What is your focus today? Joy comes when it is Jesus first, others second…then you.

Kay Arthur

We can't do everything, but can we do anything more valuable than invest ourselves in another?

Elisabeth Elliot

The measure of a life, after all, is not its duration but its donation.

Corrie ten Boom

GOD FIRST...OTHERS SECOND...

God has given so much to you, and He wants you to share His gifts with others.

DAY 72

PRAY ABOUT YOUR DECISIONS

Now if any of you lacks wisdom, he should ask God, who gives to all generously and without criticizing, and it will be given to him. But let him ask in faith without doubting. For the doubter is like the surging sea, driven and tossed by the wind.

James 1:5-6 HCSB

Have you fervently asked God for His guidance in every aspect of your life? If so, then you're continually inviting your Creator to reveal Himself in a variety of ways. As a follower of Christ, you must do no less.

Jesus made it clear to His disciples: they should pray always. So should we. Genuine, heartfelt prayer produces powerful changes in us and in our world. When we lift our hearts to our Father in heaven, we open ourselves to a never-ending source of divine wisdom and infinite love.

Do you have questions about your future that you simply can't answer? Ask for the guidance of your Heavenly Father. Do you sincerely seek to know God's purpose for your life? Then ask Him for direction—and keep asking Him every day that you live. Whatever your need, no matter how great or small, pray about it and never lose hope. God is not just near; He is here, and He's ready to talk with you. Now!

Are you weak? Weary? Confused? Troubled? Pressured? How is your relationship with God? Is it held in its place of priority? I believe the greater the pressure, the greater your need for time alone with Him.

Kay Arthur

When there is a matter that requires definite prayer, pray until you believe God and until you can thank Him for His answer.

Hannah Whitall Smith

A prayerful heart and an obedient heart will learn, very slowly and not without sorrow, to stake everything on God Himself.

Elisabeth Elliot

Prayer is the same as the breathing of air for the lungs. Exhaling makes us get rid of our dirty air. Inhaling gives clean air. To exhale is to confess, to inhale is to be filled with the Holy Spirit.

Corrie ten Boom

GOD FIRST...OTHERS SECOND...

Prayer changes things, it changes you, and it changes other people. So pray.

DAY 73

A WORLD BRIMMING WITH TEMPTATIONS

The Lord knows how to deliver the godly out of temptations.

2 Peter 2:9 NKJV

If you stop to think about it, the cold, hard evidence is right in front of your eyes: you live in a temptation-filled world. The devil is out on the street, hard at work, causing pain and heartache in more ways than ever before. Here in the 21st century, the bad guys are working around the clock to lead you astray. That's why you must remain vigilant.

In a letter to believers, Peter offered a stern warning: "Your adversary, the devil, prowls around like a roaring lion, seeking someone to devour" (1 Peter 5:8 NASB). What was true in New Testament times is equally true in our own. Satan tempts his prey and then devours them. As believing Christians, we must beware. And, if we seek righteousness in our own lives, we must earnestly wrap ourselves in the protection of God's Holy Word. When we do, we are secure.

Flee temptation without leaving a forwarding address.

Barbara Johnson

Because Christ has faced our every temptation without sin, we never face a temptation that has no door of escape.

Beth Moore

There is sharp necessity for giving Christ absolute obedience. The devil bids for our complete self-will. To whatever extent we give this self-will the right to be master over our lives, we are, to an extent, giving Satan a toehold.

Catherine Marshall

Lord, what joy to know that Your powers are so much greater than those of the enemy.

Corrie ten Boom

We, as God's people, are not only to stay far away from sin and sinners who would entice us, but we are to be so like our God that we mourn over sin.

Kay Arthur

GOD FIRST...OTHERS SECOND...

Because you live in a temptation-filled world, you must guard your eyes, your thoughts, and your heart—all day, every day.

DAY 74

LOVE ONE ANOTHER

This is My commandment, that you love one another as I have loved you.

John 15:12 NKJV

As a woman, you know the profound love that you hold in your heart for your own family and friends. As a child of God, you can only imagine the infinite love that your Heavenly Father holds for you.

God made you in His own image and gave you salvation through the person of His Son Jesus Christ. And now, precisely because you are a wondrous creation treasured by God, a question presents itself: What will you do in response to the Creator's love? Will you ignore it or embrace it? Will you return it or neglect it? That decision, of course, is yours and yours alone.

When you embrace God's love, your life's purpose is forever changed. When you embrace God's love, you will feel differently about yourself, your neighbors, your family, and your world. More importantly, you will share God's message—and His love—with others.

Your Heavenly Father—a God of infinite love and mercy—is waiting to embrace you with open arms. Accept His love today and forever.

Those who abandon ship the first time it enters a storm miss the calm beyond. And the rougher the storms weathered together, the deeper and stronger real love grows.

Ruth Bell Graham

Love is an attribute of God. To love others is evidence of a genuine faith.

Kay Arthur

Love is the seed of all hope. It is the enticement to trust, to risk, to try, and to go on.

Gloria Gaither

It is when we come to the Lord in our nothingness, our powerlessness and our helplessness that He then enables us to love in a way which, without Him, would be absolutely impossible.

Elisabeth Elliot

Live your lives in love, the same sort of love which Christ gives us, and which He perfectly expressed when He gave Himself as a sacrifice to God.

Corrie ten Boom

GOD FIRST...OTHERS SECOND...

God is love, and He expects you to share His love with others.

DAY 75

CHOICES

I have set before you life and death, blessing and curse. Choose life so that you and your descendants may live, love the Lord your God, obey Him, and remain faithful to Him. For He is your life, and He will prolong your life in the land the Lord swore to give to your fathers Abraham, Isaac, and Jacob.

Deuteronomy 30:19–20 HCSB

Life is a series of decisions and choices. Each day, we make countless decisions that can bring us closer to God...or not. When we live according to God's commandments, we earn for ourselves the abundance and peace that He intends for our lives. But, when we turn our backs upon God by disobeying Him, we bring needless suffering upon ourselves and our families.

Do you seek spiritual abundance that can be yours through the person of God's only begotten Son? Then invite Christ into your heart and live according to His teachings. And, when you confront a difficult decision or a powerful temptation, seek God's wisdom and trust it. When you do, you will receive untold blessings—not only for this day, but also for all eternity.

Freedom is not the right to do what we want but the power to do what we ought.

Corrie ten Boom

I could go through this day oblivious to the miracles all around me or I could tune in and "enjoy."

Gloria Gaither

I do not know how the Spirit of Christ performs it, but He brings us choices through which we constantly change, fresh and new, into His likeness.

Joni Eareckson Tada

Every day of our lives we make choices about how we're going to live that day.

Luci Swindoll

There may be no trumpet sound or loud applause when we make a right decision, just a calm sense of resolution and peace.

Gloria Gaither

GOD FIRST...OTHERS SECOND...

Every day you make hundreds of choices . . . and the quality of those choices determines the quality of your day and your life.

DAY 76

RADICAL CONTENTMENT

I have learned to be content in whatever circumstances I am.

Philippians 4:11 HCSB

Where can you find contentment? Is it a result of wealth, or power, or beauty, or fame? Hardly. Genuine contentment springs from a peaceful spirit, a clear conscience, and a loving heart (like yours!).

Our modern world seems preoccupied with the search for happiness. We are bombarded with messages telling us that happiness depends upon the acquisition of material possessions. These messages are false. Enduring peace is not the result of our acquisitions; it is the inevitable result of our dispositions. If we don't find contentment within ourselves, we will never find it outside ourselves.

Thus the search for contentment is an internal quest, an exploration of the heart, mind, and soul. You can find contentment—indeed you will find it—if you simply look in the right places. And the best time to start looking in those places is now.

When we do what is right, we have contentment, peace, and happiness.

Beverly LaHaye

Father and Mother lived on the edge of poverty, and yet their contentment was not dependent upon their surroundings. Their relationship to each other and to the Lord gave them strength and happiness.

Corrie ten Boom

I believe that in every time and place it is within our power to acquiesce in the will of God—and what peace it brings to do so!

Elisabeth Elliot

The key to contentment is to consider. Consider who you are and be satisfied with that. Consider what you have and be satisfied with that. Consider what God's doing and be satisfied with that.

Luci Swindoll

GOD FIRST...OTHERS SECOND...

God offers you His peace, His protection, and His promises. If you accept these gifts, you will be content.

DAY 77

MAKING THE MOST OF WHATEVER COMES

A man's heart plans his way, but the Lord determines his steps.

Proverbs 16:9 HCSB

Sometimes, we must accept life on its terms, not our own. Life has a way of unfolding, not as we will, but as it will. And sometimes, there is precious little we can do to change things.

When events transpire that are beyond our control, we have a choice: we can either learn the art of acceptance, or we can make ourselves miserable as we struggle to change the unchangeable.

We must entrust the things we cannot change to God. Once we have done so, we can prayerfully and faithfully tackle the important work that He has placed before us: doing something about the things we can change . . . and doing it sooner rather than later.

Can you summon the courage and the wisdom to accept life on its own terms? If so, you'll most certainly be rewarded for your good judgment.

Two words will help you cope when you run low on hope: accept and trust.

Charles Swindoll

It is always possible to do the will of God. In every place and time it is within our power to acquiesce in the will of God.

Elisabeth Elliot

We must meet our disappointments, our persecutions, our malicious enemies, our provoking friends, our trials and temptations of every sort, with an attitude of surrender and trust. We must spread our wings and "mount up" to the "heavenly places in Christ" above them all, where they will lose their power to harm or distress us.

Hannah Whitall Smith

The one true way of dying to self is the way of patience, meekness, humility, and resignation to God.

Andrew Murray

GOD FIRST...OTHERS SECOND...

When you encounter situations that you cannot change, you must learn the wisdom of acceptance . . . and you must learn to trust God.

DAY 78

THE POWER OF ENCOURAGEMENT

Patience and encouragement come from God. And I pray that God will help you all agree with each other the way Christ Jesus wants.

Romans 15:5 NCV

Are you a woman who is a continuing source of encouragement to your family and friends? Hopefully so. After all, one of the reasons that God put you here is to serve and encourage other people—starting with the people who live under your roof.

In his letter to the Ephesians, Paul writes, "Do not let any unwholesome talk come out of your mouths, but only what is helpful for building others up according to their needs, that it may benefit those who listen" (4:29 NIV). This passage reminds us that, as Christians, we are instructed to choose our words carefully so as to build others up through wholesome, honest encouragement. How can we build others up? By celebrating their victories and their accomplishments. As the old saying goes, "When someone does something good, applaud—you'll make two people happy."

Today, look for the good in others and celebrate the good that you find. When you do, you'll be a powerful force of encouragement in your corner of the world . . . and a worthy servant to your God.

Always stay connected to people and seek out things that bring you joy. Dream with abandon. Pray confidently.

Barbara Johnson

A single word, if spoken in a friendly spirit, may be sufficient to turn one from dangerous error.

Fanny Crosby

The glory of friendship is not the outstretched hand, or the kindly smile, or the joy of companionship. It is the spiritual inspiration that comes to one when he discovers that someone else believes in him and is willing to trust him with his friendship.

Corrie ten Boom

GOD FIRST...OTHERS SECOND...

God's Word encourages you to encourage others.

DAY 79

PUT FAITH ABOVE FEELINGS

Now the just shall live by faith.

Hebrews 10:38 NKJV

Who is in charge of your emotions? Is it you, or have you formed the unfortunate habit of letting other people—or troubling situations—determine the quality of your thoughts and the direction of your day? If you're wise—and if you'd like to build a better life for yourself and your loved ones—you'll learn to control your emotions before your emotions control you.

Human emotions are highly variable, decidedly unpredictable, and often unreliable. Our emotions are like the weather, only far more fickle. So we must learn to live by faith, not by the ups and downs of our own emotional roller coasters.

Sometime during this day, you will probably be gripped by a strong negative feeling. Distrust it. Reign it in. Test it. And turn it over to God. Your emotions will inevitably change; God will not. So trust Him completely as you watch those negative feelings slowly evaporate into thin air—which, of course, they will.

I may no longer depend on pleasant impulses to bring me before the Lord. I must rather respond to principles I know to be right, whether I feel them to be enjoyable or not.

Jim Elliot

The only serious mistake we can make is the mistake that Psalm 121 prevents: the mistake of supposing that God's interest in us waxes and wanes in response to our spiritual temperature.

Eugene Peterson

Before you can dry another's tears, you too must weep.

Barbara Johnson

Don't bother much about your feelings. When they are humble, loving, brave, give thanks for them; when they are conceited, selfish, cowardly, ask to have them altered. In neither case are they you, but only a thing that happens to you. What matters is your intentions and your behavior.

C. S. Lewis

GOD FIRST...OTHERS SECOND...

Here are the facts: God's love is real; His peace is real; His support is real. Don't ever let your emotions obscure these facts.

DAY 80

RETURN GOD'S LOVE BY SHARING IT

Dear friends, if God loved us in this way, we also must love one another.

1 John 4:11 HCSB

Because God's power is limitless, it is far beyond the comprehension of mortal minds. But even though we cannot fully understand the heart of God, we can be open to God's love.

God's ability to love is not burdened by temporal boundaries or by earthly limitations. The love that flows from the heart of God is infinite—and today presents yet another opportunity to celebrate that love.

You are a glorious creation, a unique individual, a beautiful example of God's handiwork. God's love for you is limitless. Accept that love, acknowledge it, and be grateful.

Snuggle in God's arms. When you are hurting, when you feel lonely or left out, let Him cradle you, comfort you, reassure you of His all-sufficient power and love.

Kay Arthur

The fact is, God no longer deals with us in judgment but in mercy. If people got what they deserved, this old planet would have ripped apart at the seams centuries ago. Praise God that because of His great love "we are not consumed, for his compassions never fail" (Lam. 3:22).

Joni Eareckson Tada

Being loved by Him whose opinion matters most gives us the security to risk loving, too—even loving ourselves.

Gloria Gaither

There is no pit so deep that God's love is not deeper still.

Corrie ten Boom

GOD FIRST...OTHERS SECOND...

When all else fails, God's love does not. You can always depend upon God's love . . . and He is always your ultimate protection.

DAY 81

CHOOSING TO STAND UP FOR YOUR BELIEFS

You love Him, though you have not seen Him. And though not seeing Him now, you believe in Him and rejoice with inexpressible and glorious joy, because you are receiving the goal of your faith, the salvation of your souls.

1 Peter 1:8-9 HCSB

We must do our best to make sure that our actions are accurate reflections of our beliefs. Our theology must be demonstrated, not only by our words but, more importantly, by our actions. In short, we should be practical women, quick to act upon the beliefs that we hold most dear.

We may proclaim our beliefs to our hearts' content, but our proclamations will mean nothing—to others or to ourselves—unless we accompany our words with deeds that match. The sermons that we live are far more compelling than the ones we preach.

Like it or not, your life is an accurate reflection of your creed. If this fact gives you cause for concern, don't bother talking about the changes that you intend to make—make them. Now.

Jesus taught that the evidence that confirms our leaps of faith comes after we risk believing, not before.

Gloria Gaither

Faith sees the invisible, believes the unbelievable, and receives the impossible.

Corrie ten Boom

You can better understand the 23rd Psalm when you are acquainted with The Shepherd.

Anonymous

Every man must do two things alone; he must do his own believing and his own dying.

Martin Luther

Understanding is the reward of faith. Therefore, seek not to understand that you may believe, but believe that you may understand.

St. Augustine

GOD FIRST...OTHERS SECOND...

When you live in accordance with your beliefs, God will guide your steps and protect your heart.

DAY 82

PRAY FOR PERSPECTIVE

All I'm doing right now, friends, is showing how these things pertain to Apollos and me so that you will learn restraint and not rush into making judgments without knowing all the facts. It is important to look at things from God's point of view. I would rather not see you inflating or deflating reputations based on mere hearsay.

1 Corinthians 4:6 MSG

If a temporary loss of perspective has left you worried, exhausted, or both, it's time to readjust your thought patterns. Negative thoughts are habit-forming; thankfully, so are positive ones. With practice, you can form the habit of focusing on God's priorities and your own possibilities. When you do, you'll soon discover that you will spend less time fretting about your challenges and more time praising God for His gifts.

When you call upon the Lord and prayerfully seek His will, He will give you wisdom and perspective. When you make God's priorities your priorities, He will direct your steps and calm your fears. So today and every day hereafter, pray for a sense of balance and perspective. And remember: no problems are too big for God—and that includes yours.

Attitude is the mind's paintbrush; it can color any situation.

Barbara Johnson

Like a shadow declining swiftly…away…like the dew of the morning gone with the heat of the day; like the wind in the treetops, like a wave of the sea, so are our lives on earth when seen in light of eternity.

Ruth Bell Graham

Instead of being frustrated and overwhelmed by all that is going on in our world, go to the Lord and ask Him to give you His eternal perspective.

Kay Arthur

The proper perspective creates within us a spirit of reaching outside of ourselves with joy and enthusiasm.

Luci Swindoll

GOD FIRST...OTHERS SECOND...

When you focus on the world, you lose perspective. When you focus on God's promises, you gain clearer perspective.

DAY 83

WHEN MOUNTAINS NEED MOVING

I assure you: If anyone says to this mountain, "Be lifted up and thrown into the sea," and does not doubt in his heart, but believes that what he says will happen, it will be done for him.

Mark 11:23 HCSB

When a suffering woman sought healing by simply touching the hem of His garment, Jesus turned and said, "Daughter, be of good comfort; thy faith hath made thee whole" (Matthew 9:22 KJV). We, too, can be made whole when we place our faith completely and unwaveringly in the person of Jesus Christ.

Concentration camp survivor Corrie ten Boom relied on faith during her ten months of imprisonment and torture. Later, despite the fact that four of her family members had died in Nazi death camps, Corrie's faith was unshaken. She wrote, "There is no pit so deep that God's love is not deeper still." Christians take note: Genuine faith in God means faith in all circumstances, happy or sad, joyful or tragic.

If your faith is being tested to the point of breaking, know that your Savior is near. If you reach out to Him in faith, He will give you peace and heal your broken spirit. Be content to touch even the smallest fragment of the Master's garment, and He will make you whole.

Faith is seeing light with the eyes of your heart, when the eyes of your body see only darkness.

Barbara Johnson

Grace calls you to get up, throw off your blanket of helplessness, and to move on through life in faith.

Kay Arthur

Faith does not concern itself with the entire journey. One step is enough.

Mrs. Charles E. Cowman

If God chooses to remain silent, faith is content.

Ruth Bell Graham

GOD FIRST...OTHERS SECOND...

If your faith is strong enough, you and God—working together —can move mountains.

DAY 84

WORRY LESS

Don't worry about anything, but in everything, through prayer and petition with thanksgiving, let your requests be made known to God.

Philippians 4:6 HCSB

If you are like most women, it is simply a fact of life: from time to time, you worry. You worry about health, about finances, about safety, about relationships, about family, and about countless other challenges of life, some great and some small. Where is the best place to take your worries? Take them to God. Take your troubles to Him, and your fears, and your sorrows.

Barbara Johnson correctly observed, "Worry is the senseless process of cluttering up tomorrow's opportunities with leftover problems from today." So if you'd like to make the most out of this day (and every one hereafter), turn your worries over to a Power greater than yourself . . . and spend your valuable time and energy solving the problems you can fix . . . while trusting God to do the rest.

This life of faith, then, consists in just this—being a child in the Father's house. Let the ways of childish confidence and freedom from care, which so please you and win your heart when you observe your own little ones, teach you what you should be in your attitude toward God.

Hannah Whitall Smith

Today is mine. Tomorrow is none of my business. If I peer anxiously into the fog of the future, I will strain my spiritual eyes so that I will not see clearly what is required of me now.

Elisabeth Elliott

Worries carry responsibilities that belong to God, not to you. Worry does not enable us to escape evil; it makes us unfit to cope with it when it comes.

Corrie ten Boom

GOD FIRST...OTHERS SECOND...

Work hard, pray harder, and if you have any worries, take them to God—and leave them there.

DAY 85

WHO RULES?

Can you search out the deep things of God? Can you find out the limits of the Almighty? They are higher than heaven—what can you do? Deeper than Sheol—what can you know? Their measure is longer than the earth and broader than the sea.

Job 11:7-9 NKJV

God is sovereign. He reigns over the entire universe and He reigns over your little corner of that universe. Your challenge is to recognize God's sovereignty, to live in accordance with His commandments, and to trust His promises. Sometimes, of course, these tasks are easier said than done.

Your Heavenly Father may not always reveal Himself as quickly (or as clearly) as you would like. But rest assured: God is in control, God is here, and God intends to use you in wonderful, unexpected ways. He desires to lead you along a path of His choosing. Your challenge is to watch, to listen, to learn . . . and to follow. Today.

There is something incredibly comforting about knowing that the Creator is in control of your life.

Lisa Whelchel

Our God is the sovereign Creator of the universe! He loves us as His own children and has provided every good thing we have; He is worthy of our praise every moment.

Shirley Dobson

Nothing happens by happenstance. I am not in the hands of fate, nor am I the victim of man's whims or the devil's ploys. There is One who sits above man, above Satan, and above all heavenly hosts as the ultimate authority of all the universe. That One is my God and my Father!

Kay Arthur

Every experience God gives us, every person he brings into our lives, is the perfect preparation for the future that only he can see.

Corrie ten Boom

GOD FIRST...OTHERS SECOND...

God is in control of our world . . . and your world.

DAY 86

CONTAGIOUS CHRISTIANITY

Therefore, everyone who will acknowledge Me before men, I will also acknowledge him before My Father in heaven.

Matthew 10:32 HCSB

Genuine, heartfelt Christianity can be highly contagious. When you've experienced the transforming power of God's love, you feel the need to share the Good News of His only begotten Son. So, whether you realize it or not, you can be sure that you are being led to share the story of your faith with family, with friends, and with the world.

Every believer, including you, bears responsibility for sharing God's Good News. And it is important to remember that you share your testimony through words and actions, but not necessarily in that order.

Today, don't be bashful or timid: Talk about Jesus and, while you're at it, show the world what it really means to follow Him. After all, the fields are ripe for the harvest, time is short, and the workers are surprisingly few. So please share your story today because tomorrow may indeed be too late.

The Christian lifestyle is not one of legalistic do's and don'ts, but one that is positive, attractive, and joyful.

Vonette Bright

To be a Christian means to forgive the inexcusable, because God has forgiven the inexcusable in you.

C. S. Lewis

The Holy Spirit testifies of Jesus. So when you are filled with the Holy Spirit, you speak about our Lord and really live to His honor.

Corrie ten Boom

Christianity, in its purest form, is nothing more than seeing Jesus. Christian service, in its purest form, is nothing more than imitating him who we see. To see his Majesty and to imitate him...that is the sum of Christianity.

Max Lucado

GOD FIRST...OTHERS SECOND...

If you want to be more like Jesus . . . follow in His footsteps every day, obey His commandments every day, and share His never-ending love—every day.

DAY 87

BITTERNESS PUTS DISTANCE BETWEEN YOU AND GOD

Hatred stirs up conflicts, but love covers all offenses.

Proverbs 10:12 HCSB

Are you mired in the quicksand of bitterness or regret? If so, it's time to free yourself from the mire. The world holds few if any rewards for those who remain angrily focused upon the past. Still, the act of forgiveness is difficult for all but the most saintly men and women.

Being frail, fallible, imperfect human beings, most of us are quick to anger, quick to blame, slow to forgive, and even slower to forget. Yet we know that it's best to forgive others, just as we, too, have been forgiven.

If there exists even one person—including yourself—against whom you still harbor bitter feelings, it's time to forgive and move on. Bitterness, and regret are not part of God's plan for you, but God won't force you to forgive others. It's a job that only you can finish, and the sooner you finish it, the better.

Bitterness is the price we charge ourselves for being unwilling to forgive.

Marie T. Freeman

Forgiveness is the key that unlocks the door of resentment and the handcuffs of hate. It is a power that breaks the chains of bitterness and the shackles of selfishness.

Corrie ten Boom

Bitterness is a spiritual cancer, a rapidly growing malignancy that can consume your life. Bitterness cannot be ignored but must be healed at the very core, and only Christ can heal bitterness.

Beth Moore

Grudges are like hand grenades; it is wise to release them before they destroy you.

Barbara Johnson

GOD FIRST...OTHERS SECOND...

You can never fully enjoy the present if you're bitter about the past. Instead of living in the past, make peace with it . . . and move on.

DAY 88

TACKLING TOUGH TIMES

God is our refuge and strength, a very present help in trouble.

Psalm 46:1 NKJV

Women of every generation have experienced adversity, and this generation is no different. But, today's women face challenges that previous generations could have scarcely imagined. Thankfully, although the world continues to change, God's love remains constant. And, He remains ready to comfort us and strengthen us whenever we turn to Him.

Psalm 147 promises, "He heals the brokenhearted, and binds their wounds" (v. 3). When we are troubled, we must call upon God, and, in His own time and according to His own plan, He will heal us.

If you are like most women, it is simply a fact of life: from time to time, you worry. You worry about health, about finances, about safety, about relationships, about family, and about countless other challenges of life, some great and some small. Where is the best place to take your worries? Take them to God. Take your troubles to Him, and your fears, and your sorrows. Seek protection from the One who cannot be moved.

Often God shuts a door in our face so that he can open the door through which he wants us to go.

Catherine Marshall

We all go through pain and sorrow, but the presence of God, like a warm, comforting blanket, can shield us and protect us, and allow the deep inner joy to surface, even in the most devastating circumstances.

Barbara Johnson

Often the trials we mourn are really gateways into the good things we long for.

Hannah Whitall Smith

Recently I've been learning that life comes down to this: God is in everything. Regardless of what difficulties I am experiencing at the moment, or what things aren't as would like them to be, I look at the circumstances and say, "Lord, what are you trying to teach me?"

Catherine Marshall

GOD FIRST...OTHERS SECOND...

When times are tough, you should guard your heart by turning it over to God.

DAY 89

PRAY EARLY AND OFTEN

Rejoice always! Pray constantly. Give thanks in everything, for this is God's will for you in Christ Jesus.

1 Thessalonians 5:16-18 HCSB

As the old saying goes, if it's big enough to worry about, it's big enough to pray about. Yet sometimes, we don't pray about the specific details of our lives. Instead, we may offer general prayers that are decidedly heavy on platitudes and decidedly light on particulars.

The next time you pray, try this: be very specific about the things you ask God to do. Of course God already knows precisely what you need—He knows infinitely more about your life than you do—but you need the experience of talking to your Creator in honest, unambiguous language.

So today, don't be vague with God. Tell Him exactly what you need. He doesn't need to hear the details, but you do.

What God gives in answer to our prayers will always be the thing we most urgently need, and it will always be sufficient.

Elisabeth Elliot

Your family and friends need your prayers and you need theirs. And God wants to hear those prayers. So what are you waiting for?

Marie T. Freeman

God says we don't need to be anxious about anything; we just need to pray about everything.

Stormie Omartian

The center of power is not to be found in summit meetings or in peace conferences. It is not in Peking or Washington or the United Nations, but rather where a child of God prays in the power of the Spirit for God's will to be done in her life, in her home, and in the world around her.

Ruth Bell Graham

GOD FIRST...OTHERS SECOND...

There's no corner of your life that's too unimportant to pray about, so pray about everything.

DAY 90

RADICAL CHANGE
REQUIRES OBEDIENCE

Not everyone who says to Me, "Lord, Lord!" will enter the kingdom of heaven, but the one who does the will of My Father in heaven.

Matthew 7:21 HCSB

God's laws are eternal and unchanging: obedience leads to abundance and joy; disobedience leads to disaster. God has given us a guidebook for righteous living called the Holy Bible. If we trust God's Word and live by it, we are blessed. But, if we choose to ignore God's commandments, the results are as predictable as they are tragic.

Life is a series of decisions and choices. Each day, we make countless decisions that can bring us closer to God… or not. When we live according to God's commandments, we earn for ourselves the abundance and peace that He intends for our lives.

Do you seek God's peace and His blessings? Then obey Him. When you're faced with a difficult choice or a powerful temptation, seek God's counsel and trust the counsel He gives. Invite God into your heart and live according to His commandments. When you do, you will be blessed today, and tomorrow, and forever.

Let us never suppose that obedience is impossible or that holiness is meant only for a select few. Our Shepherd leads us in paths of righteousness—not for our name's sake but for His.

Elisabeth Elliot

I don't always like His decisions, but when I choose to obey Him, the act of obedience still "counts" with Him even if I'm not thrilled about it.

Beth Moore

The cross that Jesus commands you and me to carry is the cross of submissive obedience to the will of God, even when His will includes suffering and hardship and things we don't want to do.

Anne Graham Lotz

Jesus is Victor. Calvary is the place of victory. Obedience is the pathway of victory. Bible study and prayer is the preparation for victory.

Corrie ten Boom

GOD FIRST...OTHERS SECOND...

When you are obedient to God, you are secure; when you are not, you are not.

DAY 91

RADICAL COURAGE

Be strong and courageous, and do the work. Don't be afraid or discouraged, for the Lord God, my God, is with you. He won't leave you or forsake you.

1 Chronicles 28:20 HCSB

Christians have every reason to live courageously. After all, the ultimate battle has already been fought and won on the cross at Calvary. But, even dedicated followers of Christ may find their courage tested by the inevitable disappointments and tragedies that occur in the lives of believers and non-believers alike.

Every human life is a tapestry of events: some wonderful, some not-so-wonderful, and some downright disheartening. When the storm clouds form overhead and we find ourselves wandering through the dark valley of despair, our faith is stretched, sometimes to the breaking point. But as believers, we can be comforted: Wherever we find ourselves, whether at the top of the mountain or the depths of the valley, God is there, and because He cares for us, we can live courageously.

The next time you find yourself in a fear-provoking situation, remember that God is as near as your next breath, and remember that He offers salvation to His children. He is your shield and your strength; He is your protector and your deliverer. Call upon Him in your hour of need and then be comforted. Whatever your challenge, whatever your trouble, God can handle it. And will.

Just as courage is faith in good, so discouragement is faith in evil, and, while courage opens the door to good, discouragement opens it to evil.

Hannah Whitall Smith

What is courage? It is the ability to be strong in trust, in conviction, in obedience. To be courageous is to step out in faith—to trust and obey, no matter what.

Kay Arthur

With each new experience of letting God be in control, we gain courage and reinforcement for daring to do it again and again.

Gloria Gaither

GOD FIRST...OTHERS SECOND...

If you trust God completely and without reservation, you have every reason on earth—and in heaven—to live courageously. And that's precisely what you should do.

DAY 92

ESTABLISH A GROWING RELATIONSHIP WITH JESUS

But whoever keeps His word, truly in him the love of God is perfected. This is how we know we are in Him: the one who says he remains in Him should walk just as He walked.

1 John 2:5-6 HCSB

The 19th-century writer Hannah Whitall Smith observed, "The crucial question for each of us is this: What do you think of Jesus, and do you yet have a personal acquaintance with Him?" Indeed, the answer to that question determines the quality, the course, and the direction of our lives today and for all eternity.

The old familiar hymn begins, "What a friend we have in Jesus...." No truer words were ever penned. Jesus is the sovereign Friend and ultimate Savior of mankind. Christ showed enduring love for His believers by willingly sacrificing His own life so that we might have eternal life. Now, it is our turn to become His friend.

Let us love our Savior, praise Him, and share His message of salvation with our neighbors and with the world. When we do, we demonstrate that our acquaintance with the Master is not a passing fancy; it is, instead, the cornerstone and the touchstone of our lives.

Tell me the story of Jesus. Write on my heart every word.
Tell me the story most precious, sweetest that ever was
heard.

Fanny Crosby

Jesus makes God visible. But that truth does not make Him
somehow less than God. He is equally supreme with God.

Anne Graham Lotz

Major on Jesus Christ. Make Him the preeminent One
in your life. You have all things in Him, with Him, and
through Him—and nothing is greater than that.

Warren Wiersbe

When we are in a situation where Jesus is all we have, we
soon discover he is all we really need.

Gigi Graham Tchividjian

In your greatest weakness, turn to your greatest strength,
Jesus, and hear Him say, "My grace is sufficient for you, for
My strength is made perfect in weakness."

Lisa Whelchel

GOD FIRST...OTHERS SECOND...

Jesus is the light of the world. God wants Him to be the
light of your life.

DAY 93

EXPERIENCING SILENCE

Be still, and know that I am God.

Psalm 46:10 NKJV

The world seems to grow louder day by day, and our senses seem to be invaded at every turn. If we allow the distractions of a clamorous society to separate us from God's peace, we do ourselves a profound disservice. Our task, as dutiful believers, is to carve out moments of silence in a world filled with noise.

If we are to maintain righteous minds and compassionate hearts, we must take time each day for prayer and for meditation. We must make ourselves still in the presence of our Creator. We must quiet our minds and our hearts so that we might sense God's will and His love.

Has the busy pace of life robbed you of the peace that God has promised? If so, it's time to reorder your priorities and your life. Nothing is more important than the time you spend with your Heavenly Father. So be still and claim the inner peace that is found in the silent moments you spend with God.

Let your loneliness be transformed into a holy aloneness. Sit still before the Lord. Remember Naomi's word to Ruth: "Sit still, my daughter, until you see how the matter will fall."

Elisabeth Elliot

Because Jesus Christ is our Great High Priest, not only can we approach God without a human "go-between," we can also hear and learn from God in some sacred moments without one.

Beth Moore

In the soul-searching of our lives, we are to stay quiet so we can hear Him say all that He wants to say to us in our hearts.

Charles Swindoll

It is in that stillness that the Voice will be heard, the only voice in all the universe that speaks peace to the deepest part of us.

Elisabeth Elliot

GOD FIRST...OTHERS SECOND...

Spend a few moments each day in silence. You owe it to your Creator . . . and to yourself.

DAY 94

GOD'S TIMETABLE

He has made everything appropriate in its time. He has also put eternity in their hearts, but man cannot discover the work God has done from beginning to end.

Ecclesiastes 3:11 HCSB

If you sincerely seek to be a woman of faith, then you must learn to trust God's timing. You will be sorely tempted, however, to do otherwise. Because you are a fallible human being, you are impatient for things to happen. But, God knows better.

God has created a world that unfolds according to His own timetable, not ours . . . thank goodness! We mortals might make a terrible mess of things. God does not.

God's plan does not always happen in the way that we would like or at the time of our own choosing. Our task—as believing Christians who trust in a benevolent, all-knowing Father—is to wait patiently for God to reveal Himself. And reveal Himself He will. Always. But until God's perfect plan is made known, we must walk in faith and never lose hope. And we must continue to trust Him. Always.

By his wisdom, he orders his delays so that they prove to be far better than our hurries.

C. H. Spurgeon

When we read of the great Biblical leaders, we see that it was not uncommon for God to ask them to wait, not just a day or two, but for years, until God was ready for them to act.

Gloria Gaither

Waiting on God brings us to the journey's end quicker than our feet.

Mrs. Charles E. Cowman

He whose attitude towards Christ is correct does indeed ask "in His Name" and receives what he asks for if it is something which does not stand in the way of his salvation. He gets it, however, only when he ought to receive it, for certain things are not refused us, but their granting is delayed to a fitting time.

St. Augustine

GOD FIRST...OTHERS SECOND...

You don't know precisely what you need—or when you need it—but God does. So trust His timing.

DAY 95

DO YOU BELIEVE IN MIRACLES?

You are the God who works wonders; You revealed Your strength among the peoples.

Psalm 77:14 HCSB

If you haven't seen any of God's miracles lately, you haven't been looking. Throughout history the Creator has intervened in the course of human events in ways that cannot be explained by science or human rationale. And He's still doing so today.

God's miracles are not limited to special occasions, nor are they witnessed by a select few. God is crafting His wonders all around us: the miracle of the birth of a new baby; the miracle of a world renewing itself with every sunrise; the miracle of lives transformed by God's love and grace. Each day, God's handiwork is evident for all to see and experience.

Today, seize the opportunity to inspect God's hand at work. His miracles come in a variety of shapes and sizes, so keep your eyes and your heart open. Be watchful, and you'll soon be amazed.

When we face an impossible situation, all self-reliance and self-confidence must melt away; we must be totally dependent on Him for the resources.

Anne Graham Lotz

There is Someone who makes possible what seems completely impossible.

Catherine Marshall

Are you looking for a miracle? If you keep your eyes wide open and trust in God, you won't have to look very far.

Marie T. Freeman

I could go through this day oblivious to the miracles all around me or I could tune in and "enjoy."

Gloria Gaither

Faith means believing in realities that go beyond sense and sight. It is the awareness of unseen divine realities all around you.

Joni Eareckson Tada

GOD FIRST...OTHERS SECOND...

God is in the business of doing miraculous things. You should never be afraid to ask Him for a miracle.

DAY 96

BEYOND FEAR

Even when I go through the darkest valley, I fear [no] danger, for You are with me.

Psalm 23:4 HCSB

A terrible storm rose quickly on the Sea of Galilee, and the disciples were afraid. Although they had witnessed many miracles, the disciples feared for their lives, so they turned to Jesus, and He calmed the waters and the wind.

Sometimes, we, like Jesus' disciples, feel threatened by the storms of life. When we are fearful, we, too, should turn to Him for comfort and for courage.

The next time you find yourself facing a fear-provoking situation, remember that the One who calmed the wind and the waves is also your personal Savior. Then ask yourself which is stronger: your faith or your fear. The answer should be obvious. So, when the storm clouds form overhead and you find yourself being tossed on the stormy seas of life, remember this: Wherever you are, God is there, too. And, because He cares for you, you are protected.

If a person fears God, he or she has no reason to fear anything else. On the other hand, if a person does not fear God, then fear becomes a way of life.

Beth Moore

Worry is a cycle of inefficient thoughts whirling around a center of fear.

Corrie ten Boom

God shields us from most of the things we fear, but when He chooses not to shield us, He unfailingly allots grace in the measure needed.

Elisabeth Elliot

When once we are assured that God is good, then there can be nothing left to fear.

Hannah Whitall Smith

Fear and doubt are conquered by a faith that rejoices. And faith can rejoice because the promises of God are as certain as God Himself.

Kay Arthur

GOD FIRST...OTHERS SECOND...

If you're feeling fearful or anxious, you must trust God to solve the problems that are simply too big for you to solve.

DAY 97

SHARING YOUR FAITH

But sanctify the Lord God in your hearts, and always be ready to give a defense to everyone who asks you a reason for the hope that is in you.

1 Peter 3:15 HCSB

Our personal testimonies are extremely important, but sometimes, because of shyness or insecurities, we're afraid to share our experiences. And that's unfortunate.

In his second letter to Timothy, Paul shares a message to believers of every generation when he writes, "God has not given us a spirit of timidity" (1:7). Paul's meaning is clear: When sharing our beliefs, we, as Christians, must be courageous, forthright, and unashamed.

We live in a world that desperately needs the healing message of Christ Jesus. Every believer, each in his or her own way, bears responsibility for sharing the Good News of our Savior.

Billy Graham observed, "Our faith grows by expression. If we want to keep our faith, we must share it." If you are a follower of Christ, the time to express your belief in Him is now. You know how He has touched your heart; help Him do the same for others.

There are many timid souls whom we jostle morning and evening as we pass them by; but if only the kind word were spoken they might become fully persuaded.

Fanny Crosby

Your light is the truth of the Gospel message itself as well as your witness as to Who Jesus is and what He has done for you. Don't hide it.

Anne Graham Lotz

There is nothing anybody else can do that can stop God from using us. We can turn everything into a testimony.

Corrie ten Boom

Choose Jesus Christ! Deny yourself, take up the Cross, and follow Him—for the world must be shown. The world must see, in us, a discernible, visible, startling difference.

Elisabeth Elliot

GOD FIRST...OTHERS SECOND...

Whether you realize it or not, you have a profound responsibility to tell as many people as you can about the eternal life that Christ offers to those who believe in Him.

DAY 98

DON'T OVERESTIMATE THE IMPORTANCE OF APPEARANCES

Man does not see what the Lord sees, for man sees what is visible, but the Lord sees the heart.

1 Samuel 16:7 HCSB

Are you worried about keeping up appearances? And as a result, do you spend too much time, energy, or money on things that are intended to make you look good? If so, you are certainly not alone. Ours is a society that focuses intently upon appearances. We are told time and again that we can't be "too thin or too rich." But in truth, the important things in life have little to do with food, fashion, fame, or fortune.

Today, spend less time trying to please the world and more time trying to please your earthly family and your Father in heaven. Focus on pleasing your God and your loved ones, and don't worry too much about trying to impress the folks you happen to pass on the street. It takes too much energy—and too much life—to keep up appearances. So don't waste your energy or your life.

Outside appearances, things like the clothes you wear or the car you drive, are important to other people but totally unimportant to God. Trust God.

Marie T. Freeman

If the narrative of the Scriptures teaches us anything, from the serpent in the Garden to the carpenter in Nazareth, it teaches us that things are rarely what they seem, that we shouldn't be fooled by appearances.

John Eldredge

It is comfortable to know that we are responsible to God and not to man. It is a small matter to be judged of man's judgement.

Lottie Moon

Fashion is an enduring testimony to the fact that we live quite consciously before the eyes of others.

John Eldredge

GOD FIRST...OTHERS SECOND...

How you appear to other people doesn't make much difference, but how you appear to God makes all the difference.

DAY 99

LIVE ON PURPOSE

*I, therefore, the prisoner in the Lord, urge you to walk worthy
of the calling you have received.*

Ephesians 4:1 HCSB

"What on earth does God intend for me to do with my
life?" It's an easy question to ask but, for many of us, a difficult question to answer. Why? Because God's purposes
aren't always clear to us. Sometimes we wander aimlessly
in a wilderness of our own making. And sometimes, we
struggle mightily against God in an unsuccessful attempt
to find success and happiness through our own means, not
His.

If you're a woman who sincerely seeks God's guidance,
He will give it. But, He will make His revelations known
to you in a way and in a time of His choosing, not yours, so
be patient. If you prayerfully petition God and work diligently to discern His intentions, He will, in time, lead you
to a place of joyful abundance and eternal peace.

Sometimes, God's intentions will be clear to you; other times, God's plan will seem uncertain at best. But even
on those difficult days when you are unsure which way to
turn, you must never lose sight of these overriding facts:

God created you for a reason; He has important work for you to do; and He's waiting patiently for you to do it.

And the next step is up to you.

Yesterday is just experience but tomorrow is glistening with purpose—and today is the channel leading from one to the other.

Barbara Johnson

Only God's chosen task for you will ultimately satisfy. Do not wait until it is too late to realize the privilege of serving Him in His chosen position for you.

Beth Moore

In the very place where God has put us, whatever its limitations, whatever kind of work it may be, we may indeed serve the Lord Christ.

Elisabeth Elliot

GOD FIRST...OTHERS SECOND...

God has a plan for your life, a definite purpose that you can fulfill . . . or not. Your challenge is to pray for God's guidance and to follow wherever He leads.

DAY 100

THE GIFT OF ETERNAL LIFE

For God so loved the world that He gave His only begotten Son, that whoever believes in Him should not perish but have everlasting life.

John 3:16 NKJV

Eternal life is not an event that begins when you die. Eternal life begins when you invite Jesus into your heart right here on earth. So it's important to remember that God's plans for you are not limited to the ups and downs of everyday life. If you've allowed Jesus to reign over your heart, you've already begun your eternal journey.

As mere mortals, our vision for the future, like our lives here on earth, is limited. God's vision is not burdened by such limitations: His plans extend throughout all eternity.

Let us praise the Creator for His priceless gift, and let us share the Good News with all who cross our paths. We return our Father's love by accepting His grace and by sharing His message and His love. When we do, we are blessed here on earth and throughout all eternity.

Your choice to either receive or reject the Lord Jesus Christ will determine where you spend eternity.

Anne Graham Lotz

WOMEN

If you are a believer, your judgment will not determine your eternal destiny. Christ's finished work on Calvary was applied to you the moment you accepted Christ as Savior.

Beth Moore

I can still hardly believe it. I, with shriveled, bent fingers, atrophied muscles, gnarled knees, and no feeling from the shoulders down, will one day have a new body—light, bright and clothed in righteousness—powerful and dazzling.

Joni Eareckson Tada

God has promised us abundance, peace, and eternal life. These treasures are ours for the asking; all we must do is claim them. One of the great mysteries of life is why on earth do so many of us wait so very long to lay claim to God's gifts?

Marie T. Freeman

Eternity is not something that begins after you are dead. It is going on all the time. We are in it now.

Charlotte Perkins Gilman

GOD FIRST...OTHERS SECOND...

God offers you life abundant and life eternal. Accept His gift today.